AN EXPOSITORY
PREACHER'S
NOTEBOOK

AN EXPOSITORY PREACHER'S NOTEBOOK

BY

D. W. CLEVERLEY FORD

HARPER & BROTHERS
PUBLISHERS · NEW YORK

TO OLGA
my wife,

In living with whom I have learnt
the practical application of the
Christian Faith

ACKNOWLEDGMENTS

IN writing this book, I should like to express my indebtedness to my own congregation at Holy Trinity Church, Prince Consort Road, South Kensington, in serving whom I have learnt what I have given; to the Rev. Leslie Wright, Vicar of Wimbledon, who first encouraged me to publish what I have preached; to the Very Rev. George Reindorp, Provost of Southwark, who, after some lectures on Expository Preaching which he invited me to give to the clergy of Southwark, put me in touch with Mr. Leonard Cutts, whose courtesy and wise guidance in the task of publishing have been unfailing; and last, but not least, to my friend Miss June Ricardo, who has given of her spare time to type my manuscript and help correct the proofs.

7

CONTENTS

PAGE

PREFACE — The Content and Technique of
Expository Preaching 11

Part One

A COURSE OF NEW TESTAMENT SERMONS

God's Royalty: Expositions of
St. Matthew's Gospel

1. A Royal Pedigree 25
2. The King's Names 30
3. Guarding the King 36
4. The King's Temptation 41
5. The King and the Law 47
6. The King's Touch 52
7. The King's Enemies 57
8. When the King Refuses 62
9. Watching the King 67
10. Royal Religion 72

Part Two

TWO SERIES OF OLD TESTAMENT STUDIES

I. The Requirements of Leadership: Three
Old Testament Character Studies

1. Saul the Gifted 79
2. David the Spiritually-minded 89
3. Solomon the Pompous 97

9

II. The Servant of God: Four Studies on "The Servant Songs" of Isaiah

PAGE

1. The Servant's Bearing 108
2. The Servant's Equipment 117
3. The Servant's Experience 128
4. The Suffering Servant 136

Part Three

A COLLECTION OF INDIVIDUAL SERMONS

1. First Principles 147
2. How God Gives 152
3. Possessing the Land 158
4. Spoiled Clay 164
5. The Heart of Religion 169
6. The Call of God's Servant 175
7. A Window on God 181
8. The Principle of Acceptance 186
9. When Preaching is Effective 191
10. The Gospel versus Legalism 198
11. The More Excellent Way 204
12. The Human in the Divine 210
13. A Door in Heaven 216

PREFACE

The Content and Technique of Expository Preaching

EXPOSITORY preaching might almost be described as a lost art in the mid-twentieth century. This may be due to various causes—the decay of Bible Reading in the twentieth century, the fact that large numbers of the clergy have received a form of training in which the critical approach to the Bible has left them uncertain of its authority, the necessity for sermons to be short in modern times, and the fact that all preaching, and therefore expository preaching, has been under a cloud for many years.

There are at present signs of a change in this adverse climate. Largely through the Bible Reading Associations there is the beginning of a recovery of individual Bible Reading. There is also a new Biblical theology and awareness of the wholeness of the Canon of Scripture. And if sermons must still be shorter than in a more leisurely period of history, the taste for sermons can be acquired and there is, in fact, a re-emergence of the sense of the importance of the "Ministry of the Word". The 1958 Lambeth Report has encouraged this.

On account of these considerations it may be that the time for fully developed expository preaching has not yet come; but something in the direction of this form of preaching should be attempted and, in our view, can be attempted.

But what is expository preaching? It is uncovering hidden treasure. The word the disciples on the Emmaus Road used was διανοίγω, meaning "to open". The scriptures are a closed book and it is the task of the minister of Christ to open the book. He is to open up the ground and expose the treasure. This presupposes spade work.

11

Expository preaching can concern itself with any one of the following six:

(i) The whole Bible. It is possible to expose the grand sweep of God's saving acts in history (the "Heilsgeschichte") showing the unity of the scriptures.

(ii) A book of the Bible, e.g., the Book of Genesis, illustrating the way of faith as the way of safety; or St. Matthew's Gospel, showing Christ as the King.

(iii) A paragraph or chapter of the Bible, corresponding to a Sunday "lesson" at Matins or Evensong.

(iv) One verse, e.g., "The wages of sin is death but the free gift of God is eternal life in Christ Jesus our Lord."

(v) A Bible word—such as Grace, Faith, Sin, etc.

(vi) A Bible character, e.g., Saul, David, Solomon, etc.

Such expository preaching as is at present engaged in would come under category (iv). The plea here is for a style of preaching which would fit category (iii) or even (ii) or (i). Most of the sermons in this book in fact illustrate category (iii); the sermon called First Principles, p. 147, illustrates category (ii).

In passing, it needs to be said what expository preaching is not. Most emphatically it is not a lecture in scripture exegesis. Expository preaching is still preaching and as such must be addressed to the whole man expecting to move his mind, his feelings and his will. An expository sermon calls for a response, verdict or decision. There can be no possible exception to this. Nor is such preaching hanging a discourse on some text which might seem to fit. The worst example known to the writer was the Vicar who preached at the time of a General Election at a service, to which the rival Parliamentary candidates were invited, on the text "Give the more diligence to make your calling and election sure" (II Peter 1, v. 10). This is inexcusable.

The spade work which expository preaching requires involves attention to the following four disciplines:

(i) Textual criticism. A sermon can often be "lit up" by reference to a marginal reading, e.g., the marginal reading in the Greek Testament for Matthew 27, vv. 16 and 17.

(ii) Exegesis. This involves study of the best scripture commentaries. If exposition is not to become fanciful, exegesis must precede it. The first question to ask of a scripture passage is—"What in all probability did this passage mean in the mind of the writer and for those to whom it was originally written?"

(iii) Exposition. This means drawing out the principles which are latent in a scripture passage. The question may be asked—What is the difference between (ii) and (iii)? To which an illustration might be given by way of answer: an exegesis of the Epistle to the Galatians would examine St. Paul's battle with the Judaizers in the first century in Galatia, whereas an exposition would proceed to examine the relation of law to gospel as it concerns Christians in the present.

(iv) Application. There may be small justification for separating this out as a fourth point, but, forasmuch as expository preaching is still preaching, there is a necessity to apply the principles of exposition to the particular and local needs of a specific congregation.

* * *

The question may be asked—Why engage in this kind of preaching, especially in view of its difficulties? To this the answer may be given—because the Bible is the Church's treasure. It is not its only treasure, there are the sacraments; but it is its great treasure, which being the case it would be folly not to expose it. The Bible is a treasure because it records men's experience of the redeeming acts of God in history, albeit in fallible human writings. It is a primary source book. The Church has no other for the saving acts of God in Christ.

The Bible is also an inspired record. Nowadays we may not be able to believe in plenary inspiration of the scriptures, but is not I Corinthians, chapter 13, for example, inspired? And can we not in this sense believe in verbal inspiration? The truth is, the Church has an inspired book to expose and not a mere set of historical documents, and when this is incorporated into preaching there is the possibility of inspired preachers. Preaching is more likely to become inspired if it is informed by Bible language.

A second answer to the question "Why engage in expository preaching?" is "Because the sermon is part of worship". In the Church of England the worship is liturgical and the liturgy is thoroughly informed by the Bible. All the scripture passages read in a service fit the day in the Church's calendar. Expository preaching is therefore preaching which keys into worship. Thus the fault of regarding the worship as a mere preliminary is overcome, and the fault of regarding the sermon as an unimportant appendage to the worship is also overcome. The sermon should be an integral part of the worship, and the Bible is the bond lying ready to hand to make it so.

This mode of preaching also sustains the pulpit. It provides an inexhaustible fund of material of various kinds. Furthermore, it roots the teaching from the pulpit in people's minds by attaching it to pegs in them in the form of Bible stories they partly know, or at least have already heard in the "lesson". And it stabs hearers into awareness through the astonishment of seeing how an ancient Bible passage relates to modern life. This is an experience of revelation in the pew.

The method also allows the preacher to speak with an authority without which his preaching is insipid. It does this because the expository preacher is not speaking in his own name but is exposing that under whose judgment he also sits. And if the preacher is effective in his unearthing, the Bible will become for his hearers the Word of God. This is the most important reason for expository preaching. It will mean that the people in the pews are not merely offered teaching about God but will be confronted by God himself in the form of his Word. This is the true "Ministry of the Word" commended to all in the sacred ministry who at their ordination were solemnly presented with a copy of the scriptures.

Yet the fact remains that, however strong may be the arguments for expository preaching, and they are not difficult to adduce, few will be encouraged to tackle the task unless they are shown that it can be done. Because of this, and in the hope that others may be encouraged to improve upon them, the expository sermons in this book are humbly offered.

* * *

That this is a book of sermons and lectures needs to be made abundantly clear. It is not another book *about* preaching. It aims at providing expository sermon material. This is the reason for the word "Notebook" in the title. Not that the book consists of a series of jottings or outlines. The following pages contain finished sermons and lectures which have been delivered in public. But the hope is that they will provide, or suggest, material for *other* preachers' notebooks. No man can effectively preach another's sermons and those published in this book are no exception, they cannot and must not be preached as they stand. Their use is to suggest ideas for the expository preacher's notebook.

Possibly, however, a little more is required than simply to offer sermon material. Experience gained in lecturing on this subject tends to confirm this. Preachers wish to learn something of the technique of expository sermon preparation. They ask such questions as—"How do you select the subject for your sermon?" "Having selected the passage of scripture to expose in your sermon, how do you set about collecting material?" "Must expository sermons be written out in full?" "How long does it take to prepare this kind of sermon?" "Are expository sermons 'over the heads' of the average congregation?"

Such questions ought to be answered. Since, however, sermons are essentially the result of individual and highly personal labour, they can only be answered from a personal standpoint, and this renders the answers incapable of universal application. Nevertheless, those called to preach find the hearing of such answers profitable because of the possibility

15

that in the light of them they may be able to develop their own technique.

* * *

First of all then, in preparing an expository sermon, read next Sunday's "lessons". Read them in more than one English translation, and if also in the original Hebrew or Greek, so much the better. Having done this, select that which makes the strongest appeal. The scripture which appeals most to the preacher is likely to be that which in the end will most effectively move the hearer. But if the selection is made from the Church Lectionary, the selection will reflect not *simply* the preacher's personal preference, but the teaching appropriate for the particular Sunday of the Christian year. Thus over the whole course of the year there will be a balance in the teaching.

And when the sermon is based on one of the Sunday lessons, the preacher is well advised to read that lesson himself in the course of the service of worship. It is his first battle for the minds and hearts of his congregation. If he fails in the reading of the lesson, he is likely to fail in the preaching of the expository sermon based on it. If he wins then, if he reads in an arresting fashion, being as it were caught up in the scripture, he is likely to win in the sermon. And he should be *able* to read the lesson persuasively if he has made a study of it during the preceding week, indeed he should almost know it by heart.

Having selected the passage of scripture for the expository sermon, the *second step* is to consult the standard commentaries which refer to it. It must be admitted that much that is read will be wholly unsuitable for reproduction in the sermon. This fact, however, neither invalidates the commentaries nor their use in sermon preparation. This discipline ensures that the final exposition is in alignment with reasonable exegesis, it is part of the digging process which is involved in exposing the treasures of the Bible. Exposition neglects exegesis at its peril.

16

A *third step*, and a most important one, is the collection of sermon material. How does the preacher decide what to say on the scripture passage he has selected? He may begin by asking himself why this lesson was chosen for this particular Sunday. On some occasions, such as the major festivals, the answer will be obvious; on other Sundays, however, the reason may be obscure. But before he decides that the compilers of the lectionary were stupid, he should think again —the process may provide the theme he needs for his sermon.

Another question, often productive of ideas, is to ask— Why was this Old Testament lesson chosen to be read in conjunction with this New Testament lesson? What theme have they in common? Is it a suitable subject for next Sunday? Not infrequently such lines of thought yield ideas for a sermon.

Yet another question is this—Is there a verse in this lesson or passage of scripture which (*a*) sums up its chief meaning, (*b*) could serve as a text, and (*c*) may suggest a sermon title? Furthermore, is it possible to expand the chief meaning into a number of points *from the lection*?

Since this is a most important stage in the preparation of the sermon, it may be that some illustrations will help to make the process clear.

Take, for example, the story commonly known as "The Flight into Egypt". It is found in Matthew, chapter 2, vv. 13-23—the lesson in 1959 for Epiphany I. The epitome of the account is contained in verse 13, which may therefore serve as a text for a sermon: "Herod will seek the young child to destroy him." And this in turn may suggest a title for the sermon—"Taking Care of Christ" or "Guarding the King". This theme could then be expanded or applied in three ways as follows:

(i) The Church must take care of Christ—it can lose him in ecclesiasticism, etc.

(ii) In our thinking we must take care of Christ—we can lose him through such systems as Rationalism and

17

Scientific Humanism which become "Herods" seeking to destroy him.

(iii) In our religious practice we must be disciplined, for example, in our Church-going, or we may lose Christ.

The seriousness of the matter is that in losing Christ we lose our own salvation or safety.

How this outline is expanded into a sermon can be seen on page 36 and following.

Another example could be the account of St. Paul's sermon in Antioch of Pisidia, the lesson in 1959 for Easter V. It is contained in Acts 13, vv. 26-43. The impression this sermon made is summarised in v. 42, which might therefore serve as a text: "And as they went out they besought that these words might be spoken to them the next Sabbath."

This in turn suggests a title for the sermon—"When preaching is effective" or "A sermon worth repeating"; and the theme could be expanded from the narrative and applied in the following ways: Preaching is effective when:

(i) It interprets history (vv. 26-31).
(ii) It interprets the scriptures (vv. 32-37).
(iii) It interprets human need (vv. 38-41).

How this outline may be expanded into a sermon may be seen on page 191 and following.

Almost all the other sermons contained in this book have been prepared in this fashion. In each case, a passage of scripture precedes the sermon; from this a verse has been selected which to some extent summarises the whole; and the theme suggested by this verse has been expanded into a number of points and applied.

There is a practical reason for this method. An average congregation is unable to sustain its attention throughout a verse-by-verse exposition of a passage of scripture. Such a method can be successfully attempted with a specialised audience, and no doubt the result is expository preaching proper. An illustration of this is to be found in the expositions of "The Servant Songs" of Isaiah which were given at a Diocesan Retreat for Clergy (see page 108). For most ordinary congregations, however, the exposition must group itself around one central theme. As a general rule, congregations cannot absorb more than this. Admittedly the resulting expository sermon is of a simpler kind, but it is expository, and it does captivate the pew and it does sustain the pulpit.

* * *

The three steps which have been given as part of the labour of preparing an expository sermon are peculiar to that kind of sermon. An expository sermon is not the only kind, nor the kind that should be preached every time the preacher enters the pulpit. Inasmuch, however, as an expository sermon is still a sermon, it will need that labour bestowed on it which all sermons need. It will need an introduction, something which will arrest the attention of the hearer, and yet be more than an attention-drawing device. It must bear an observable relationship to the theme of the sermon, it should in fact *introduce* the theme. By and large, introductions are of two kinds, those which begin with a story or anecdote; and those which begin with sharp, short, arresting sentences. An illustration of the first kind can be seen in the sermon on page 52 called "The King's Touch", and an illustration of the second in the sermon on page 57 called "The King's Enemies". Much labour will need to be exercised to shape these introductions. They are most important.

An expository sermon, like all sermons, should also function as part of the pastoral office. Perhaps this needs *special* emphasis in the case of an expository sermon. It is not an academic exercise. It needs a pastoral aim; and that pastoral aim can only be devised by the expository preacher who knows personally the needs of the flock committed to his care. George M. Docherty has finely expressed this in his Introduction to a volume of George Morrison's Sermons called *The Incomparable Christ* (Hodder & Stoughton, London 1959), page 10: "The man who has not visited the homes of his people, or listened to their tragic tales, sat in the dark watches of the night at a hospital bed, seen the joy of new parents, or watched the numbing silence of bereavement, has really no definitive purpose to which to preach, no goal for the good news of God. Thus the preacher with a large pastoral ministry finds he has no time to prepare for the pulpit because of the labour of pastoral work. The insoluble dilemma of the preacher is that without a congregation he cannot preach; with a large congregation he has little time to prepare. The secret in the preaching of Morrison of Wellington is that he solved this pastor-preacher tension." It is a tension the expository preacher must solve.

In expository preaching, as in all preaching, the character and personality of the preacher himself is important, but it is a subject which does not lie within the scope of this book. Yet so fundamental is it that it cannot be passed without notice. The first criterion as to whether or not an audience will attend to a speaker is to be found in the answer to the question—Who is he? It is a sobering thought. What a man is conditions the effect of what he says. It is a reminder that the preacher who exposes the Word of God must himself be a man of God.

He will also have a distinctive personality. He should not be at pains to hide this. If the definition by Phillips Brooks of real preaching is correct, namely that it is "truth through personality", the preacher who consistently refuses to reveal his personality must end by being less effective. A man's work will indicate the man. Because of this, no attempt has been made in the sermons that follow to suppress the clues which some (clergy and ministers?) will find, revealing the preacher as an Anglican, adopting an ecclesiastical position on the evangelical side of centre, and a post-Barthian liberal in theological thought. These and perhaps more interesting (and intelligible!) personal hints have been left bare. A sermon is a declaration of the Word of God by a *particular* man.

* * *

Ought expository sermons to be written out in full? That those published in this book have been written out in full is obvious. They have in fact been written, re-written and re-written again. Perhaps more than ten hours a piece have been spent on their preparation. But they have not been read in the pulpit, they have been preached; indeed, after the expenditure of many hours on a sermon manuscript, a preacher can almost preach without it. And when after such preparation he preaches in this way, he is free from the necessity to be feeling for the appropriate word or phrase and is able to concentrate entirely on delivery. Being a master of his subject, he will preach with authority, conviction and confidence, and without these qualities no preaching is likely to be effective.

* * *

Is the recovery of the art of expository preaching possible to-day? Is it possible in the presence of our modern critical approach to the scriptures? Is it possible in view of the comparative ignorance of the average member of Christian congregations of the contents of the Bible? It is possible. This is what the sermons that follow in this book attempt to show. The final answer, however, does not lie with the provision of sermon material, however engaging; nor with the teaching of technique, however sound. It lies with the preacher who in "digging" to expose the scriptures seeks the aid of Him who takes the things of Christ and shows them unto men (John, chapter 16, v. 14), namely the Spirit of God Himself, the Interpreter.

PART ONE

A COURSE OF NEW TESTAMENT SERMONS

God's Royalty: Expositions of St. Matthew's Gospel

1. A ROYAL PEDIGREE

ST. MATTHEW, CHAPTER I, VV. I-17

The book of the generation of Jesus Christ, the son of David, the son of Abraham.

Abraham begat Isaac; and Isaac begat Jacob; and Jacob begat Judah and his brethren; and Judah begat Perez and Zerah of Tamar; and Perez begat Hezron; and Hezron begat Ram; and Ram begat Amminadab; and Amminadab begat Nahshon; and Nahshon begat Salmon; and Salmon begat Boaz of Rahab; and Boaz begat Obed of Ruth; and Obed begat Jesse; and Jesse begat David the king.

And David begat Solomon of her that had been the wife of Uriah; and Solomon begat Rehoboam; and Rehoboam begat Abijah; and Abijah begat Asa; and Asa begat Jehoshaphat; and Jehoshaphat begat Joram; and Joram begat Uzziah; and Uzziah begat Jotham; and Jotham begat Ahaz; and Ahaz begat Hezekiah; and Hezekiah begat Manasseh; and Manasseh begat Amon; and Amon begat Josiah; and Josiah begat Jechoniah and his brethren, at the time of the carrying away to Babylon.

And after the carrying away to Babylon, Jechoniah begat Shealtiel; and Shealtiel begat Zerubbabel; and Zerubbabel begat Abiud; and Abiud begat Eliakim; and Eliakim begat Azor; and Azor begat Sadoc; and Sadoc begat Achim; and Achim begat Eliud; and Eliud begat Eleazar; and Eleazar begat Matthan; and Matthan begat Jacob; and Jacob begat Joseph the husband of Mary, of whom was born Jesus, who is called Christ.

So all the generations from Abraham unto David are fourteen generations; and from David unto the carrying away to Babylon fourteen generations; and from the carrying away to Babylon unto the Christ fourteen generations.

MATTHEW 1, vv. 15, 16: . . . and Eleazar
begat Matthan; and Matthan begat Jacob; and
Jacob begat Joseph the husband of Mary, of
whom was born Jesus, who is called Christ.

I HAVE abbreviated it of course. You'd be bored to tears if
I read through the whole of the genealogy with which St.
Matthew's gospel begins. But suppose your *own* name was
in the list! Or the name of someone you knew! . . . I was looking
through some old genealogies a few weeks ago belonging to
the seventeenth century. And there I discovered names of
four or five families known to me quite well. Do you think
those tables were boring after that? They were one of the
most interesting sections of the book! . . . And that is how it
was with the genealogy at the beginning of St. Matthew's
gospel. The Jews for whom it was written *raced* their eyes
down it. So *this* is who Jesus was! These were his ancestors!
You can see it for yourself in his family tree—"The book of
the genealogy of Jesus Christ the son of David, the son of
Abraham."—St. Matthew was committing no blunder in
style when thus he began.

But what does this genealogy mean? It means first of all
that Jesus was a Jew. Do not let anyone attempt to rationalise
that fact away. It cannot be done. Jesus belonged to that
portion of Jewry which returned from exile and probably
became the Ashkenazim of Europe, the people who have
produced Einstein, Trotsky, Freud, and Marx.

But this isn't all. It means that when God became incarnate
in this world, he did not assume human flesh in the abstract;
he became part of a family, a family with a family tree, a
family with blood biologists could catalogue, a family with a
history historians could trace. There may be advantages in
such membership of a family. Glory can be inherited—but
so can dishonour. Family membership cuts two ways. So
that when God entered this world he entered in such a
fashion as to experience our problem—the family problem.

The problem of *illustrious* relations; the problem of disgraceful relations; the problem of the skeleton in the cupboard; the problem of mediocrity.

James Stalker in his book *Imago Christi* pictures the door bell ringing one night and on going out you see a stranger on the doorstep, a stranger from a strange land. You know nothing of him. He is outside the circle of your interests. He is 10,000 miles away from your spirit. But suppose he says, "Don't you know me? I'm your brother." What happens? In one step he journeys 10,000 miles. You and he are connected by an indissoluble bond; and the bond may be a golden clasp, or it may be an iron clamp burning and corroding your skin.

This is the institution called the family God entered when he took our flesh. And remember, not merely in theory, but also in practice. Jesus' brothers did not believe in him. From John, chapter 7, we can sense the animosity in the Nazareth home. And before that day, and since that day, in Judea and in Central London, upright men and women have had to endure an endless petty persecution at home worse than public opposition. *That* is what God assumed when he assumed our flesh. It has its own message this morning to any troubled at home. Christ knows what you feel, the poignancy of some family relationships, he felt it himself. . . .

* * *

" . . . and Eleazar begat Matthan; and Matthan begat Jacob; and Jacob begat Joseph the husband of Mary, of whom was born Jesus, who is called Christ." What else does this dull-looking genealogy mean? It means that when Christ entered our world, he entered a family in *circumstances calling for a defence.*

You see it isn't an ordinary family tree in Matthew, chapter 1. Four women's names occur in it. That is unusual. And more than that, the life of each woman mentioned was not without some sort of suspicion. There was Bathsheba. You all know about her! And Tamar's reputation was similar. And Rahab is bluntly called in scripture "a harlot".

27

And the fourth woman, though virtuous, wasn't even a Jewess at all, but a Moabite. Her name was Ruth. All these four women are listed as ancestresses of Jesus! Their names are *dragged* in. Why? Because when Matthew was writing his gospel he was facing Jewish opposition. Opposition which persisted in pointing the finger of scorn at the mystery surrounding Jesus' birth—"Who was his father?" And Matthew, unable to deny the strangeness of Jesus' birth, ran his finger over the long story of Hebrew history crying, "God has overruled before, God has overruled appearances before. What about Tamar! What about Bathsheba! What about Rahab! What about Ruth!"

> "Judge not the Lord by feeble sense,
> But trust him for his grace"

God is righteous; and if so the manner of the Child's birth was righteous whatever the strangeness. He was no bastard, as some Jews would have men think. And the measure of our shock when such words are used is the measure of the sordidness Christ willingly entered to come and rescue this our world.

* * *

Once more I examine this genealogy: " . . . and Eleazar begat Matthan; and Matthan begat Jacob; and Jacob begat Joseph the husband of Mary, of whom [feminine!] was born Jesus, who is called Christ."

It is an artificially constructed genealogy. There are three groups of fourteen generations, though the number is achieved in the third group only by repeating a name. No doubt the arrangement is to aid the memory. But more than this. It is to show that kingship achieved in David and lost in Jechoniah was recovered in Jesus.

What does this mean? It means that out of the complications of a family network, out of birth circumstances apparently compromising, Jesus achieved kingship. Not a kingship of this world. Not a throne on Zion's hill. But a royalty of life surpassing any that any man has seen before or since. But it is God's royalty, God's regal saintliness.

Is this challenging? It is meant to be challenging. Where we fail and excuse ourselves by pointing to our limitations of home, environment and opposition, Jesus did not fail. He exhibited the kingly life amidst all the tensions of a family network. And when on the Ascension Mount he gave the Apostles the royal commission to be his witnesses, beginning at Jerusalem (their home city), he was but commanding what he himself had achieved—a royalty of life in a family in a village.

* * *

Am I addressing myself this morning to someone worn with troubles at home? Am I addressing myself to someone beset by family problems: a marriage breaking up, a marriage broken up—some disgrace—some scandal—some skeleton? It would be a strange congregation if nothing here were known of such troubles as these. To live these days is to touch these problems. And at this point we are sensitive. That of which we should be proud is that of which we may be ashamed. And you ask me, perhaps with no expectancy in your voice, What has the Christian religion to say to such a situation as mine? My friend, it has this to say—and it will surprise you—Christ entered it. That is the gospel according to St. Matthew. Christ entered it. I haven't invented the idea. You can see it for yourself by turning to the first page of St. Matthew's gospel. The gospel begins amid the heartbreaks and splendours of a family tree. That is where Jesus began to achieve our rescue. From the place where you are; from the place where I am. That is the gospel according to St. Matthew. And the remarkable fact is, it can best be appreciated by the man looking out from a broken home. All of which cries aloud—doesn't it?—that no one need feel forsaken after this. God knows. God understands. And his Grace is free for you, whatever your need, whatever your problem.

2. THE KING'S NAMES

Now the birth of Jesus Christ was on this wise: When his mother Mary had been betrothed to Joseph, before they came together she was found with child of the Holy Ghost. And Joseph her husband, being a righteous man, and not willing to make her a public example, was minded to put her away privily. But when he thought on these things, behold, an angel of the Lord appeared unto him in a dream, saying, Joseph, thou son of David, fear not to take unto thee Mary thy wife: for that which is conceived in her is of the Holy Ghost. And she shall bring forth a son; and thou shalt call his name Jesus; for it is he that shall save his people from their sins. Now all this is come to pass, that it might be fulfilled which was spoken by the Lord through the prophet, saying,

> *Behold, the virgin shall be with child, and*
> *shall bring forth a son,*
> *And they shall call his name Immanuel;*

which is, being interpreted, God with us. And Joseph arose from his sleep, and did as the angel of the Lord commanded him, and took unto him his wife; and knew her not till she had brought forth a son: and he called his name Jesus.

MATTHEW 1, v. 23: Behold, the virgin shall be with child, and shall bring forth a son, And they shall call his name Immanuel; which is, being interpreted, God with us.

THAT takes some believing! It always has taken some believing. It took some believing when St. Matthew wrote his gospel, which is precisely *why* he wrote that second half of the first chapter, which is the subject of our consideration this morning. I go even further—it took some believing on the part of Joseph when the facts were first presented to him!

You put yourself in his shoes. He was in love with Mary. He was engaged to Mary. There was no one in his eyes at that time more desirable in all the world than Mary. But at the very time when he contemplated completing the engagement in marriage she was found to be with child, and not by himself. I say, "Put yourself in Joseph's shoes." . . .

Perhaps you complain I am being frank this morning. But the narrative is frank. And I do not think we shall grasp the poignancy of this situation unless we *are* frank. Of course Mary said, "This is God's child." I surmise Mary said it with tears, many tears. And how many times she was to experience tears! Did Joseph believe it? Let me ask you— "Would *you* believe it?" . . .

It falls to the lot of a clergyman to talk to many people about matrimonial troubles, and I always feel deeply sorry for all who come to me in these difficulties. Almost always it is a case of tension involving law and love. So it was here. Joseph should put away Mary. But Joseph loved Mary. That is enough to keep a man awake at nights. It is enough to keep a woman awake at nights. And in this situation in Galilee an engagement was considered as binding, and so could not be terminated informally. There had to be a writ of divorcement. And Joseph hated the publicity of it all. Not only for his own sake, but for Mary's, thereby showing his love. Joseph "was therefore minded" as the scripture says, "to put her away privily". She could return to her own home. There would be gossip, but better that than open repudiation in the courts.

And while the anguish burned, and Joseph's unbelievable unbelief in Mary seemed to make no sense at all of life, God spoke in Joseph's soul: "Fear not to take unto thee Mary thy wife; for that which is conceived in her is of the Holy Ghost." And that Joseph, a righteous man, married her is evidence of the truth of the narrative. But it took a word from God to establish Mary's condition as one of conception by the Holy Ghost; how could it be otherwise?

* * *

I think we shall have to look our opposers in the face on this matter. Many Jews simply believed that Mary's child was born out of wedlock, and gibes were two a penny on the subject. Recent unbelief is less vulgar. A modern view is that the prophecy in Isaiah—"Behold the virgin shall be with child, and shall bring forth a son"—is the *origin* of the idea. But the matter is not so simple. The Hebrew word translated "virgin" strictly means a woman of the age to be a mother whether married or not. It *could* be rendered "virgin", and St. Matthew clearly read it that way, but not so everybody. So it looks as if the event lit up the prophecy rather than the prophecy wishfully causing the event to be thought up.

Other critics look to oriental and hellenistic legends as parallels. Miraculous births were attributed to Pythagoras, Plato and Cæsar Augustus. Perseus was supposed to have been born from the virgin Danae by a visitation from Zeus in the form of a shower of gold. The difficulty here is that the New Testament birth narratives are thoroughly Hebrew, *no* hellenistic marks are evident, and the story is unique in making the virgin an ordinary young woman of the humbler classes.

Another line of argument is that the early Christians' opposition to the sexuality of human nature made them feel they had to invent a virgin birth if Mary's child was to be counted divine. Some early Christians certainly held these views about sexuality, which is how I think Jesus' brothers and sisters have come to be called Joseph's children and not Mary's; but this objection to the virgin birth is weakened if Mary did have children by Joseph later on, and there is St. Matthew, chapter 1, verse 25. She at least would have no reason to invent a virgin birth.

* * *

And somebody in the congregation is growing weary with all this. I am sorry, but you see we cannot have it said that Christians are such fools they accept the virgin birth uncritically. We don't. We see the difficulties. We also see the difficulties in rejecting it. And while I would not unchurch a man for reserving his judgment, I recommend as more safe taking the line the Church has taken—"conceived by the Holy Ghost, born of the Virgin Mary".

We have *history* then in the first chapter of St. Matthew's gospel, frank history. Joseph married Mary when she was three months with child. We also have apologetics in the form of defence of the event. In the third place there is interpretation. St. Matthew draws out a little the *meaning* of the event. This is done with reference to the child's names.

First we take the name Immanuel. "Behold the, virgin shall be with child, and shall bring forth a son, and they shall call his name Immanuel." It might have been simpler. It might have been Immanuish—"a man with us". Instead it is "Immanuel"—*God* with us. This is the Christian's faith epitomised. Let us be clear on this point. Our faith about the child born of Mary is not that he grew to be a good man whose teaching was inspiring and whose goodness men copied. There is very little gospel in that. And we shall have to concede the point to Montefiore that there is very little in the teaching of Jesus which cannot be paralleled in the rabbis' teaching. No, the Christian faith is that, with the birth of this child, something unique happened in history. *God* entered it; since when, looking at the great human family tree spreading its network over all the world, we can say, "Immanuel—God with us."

The Greek fathers of the Church tended to count this participation of God in the human family as itself our redemption, just as if a drop of disinfecting fluid had been allowed to purify a glass of infected water. But the notion is too mechanical. We are not microbes in stagnant water. We are men, with minds and wills and feelings. There cannot be redemption without human response as well as divine

33

initiative. But the Christian truth remains. God is with us. God is here—Immanuel. In the birth of Mary's child we see the beginning of a unique act of God "for us men and our salvation".

Opinions differ, but I expect the word Immanuel has reference to Jesus' work rather than to his nature. And this is brought out in the second interpretative word in this first chapter of St. Matthew: "Thou shall call his name Jesus for he shall save his people from their sins."

It comes as something of a surprise to people to learn that the name Jesus was common among the Jews. There was a Jesus among Our Lord's ancestors. According to one Greek manuscript, Barabbas also bore the name Jesus; and there was a Jesus in Paul's company when he wrote the Epistle to the Colossians. This seems strange at first to us when we think of our hymn:

> Jesus is the name we treasure
> Name all other names above . . .

But the truth is, when God became man he chose a name as common as Smith or Jones or Baker. God became the common man. This again is Immanuel, "God with us". And the purpose of it all is that he should save his people from their sins.

I do not myself think that Christ does this merely by being born into our world. The gospel is not "the *birth* of Jesus Christ God's son cleanseth us from all sin" but rather "the *blood* of Jesus Christ God's son cleanseth us from all sin". And the sign in which we conquer is not a cradle but a cross. But the birth is part of the redemptive process, and no sooner was Jesus born than his work was delineated: "Thou shall call his name Jesus for he shall save his people from their sins."

* * *

Have we, I wonder, grasped this truth in our congregation? Every one of us? because it is saving truth. Christians are not first of all wise men following a teacher, nor are they morally superior to their fellows in copying a saint. In the first place

34

Christians are men and women who sense their own unworthiness, yet reckon themselves safe, because of what began to take place when a virgin was with child and she brought forth a son.

I know this is revolutionary. It always has been revolutionary, and will be till the end of time. I know, too, that there is more to salvation than this. But nothing that can be said later will conflict with this basis. And if the basis is misconceived, nothing that is superimposed can possibly be in alignment. So let me reiterate the basis. This is the ground of our human soul's salvation: "Behold, the virgin shall be with child, and shall bring forth a son, and they shall call his name Immanuel; which is, being interpreted, God with us."

So you see, it is not first something which you do which saves your soul eternally, but something which God has done. "Behold, the virgin shall be with child." *That* is the beginning of the gospel. *That* is our security. Something God has done.

3. GUARDING THE KING

ST. MATTHEW, CHAPTER 2, VV. 13-23

*Now when they were departed, behold, an angel of the
Lord appeareth to Joseph in a dream, saying, Arise and take the
young child and his mother, and flee into Egypt, and be thou
there until I tell thee: for Herod will seek the young child to
destroy him. And he arose and took the young child and his
mother by night, and departed into Eygpt; and was there until
the death of Herod: that it might be fulfilled which was spoken
by the Lord through the prophet, saying, Out of Egypt did I call
my son. Then Herod, when he saw that he was mocked of the
wise men, was exceeding wroth, and sent forth, and slew all the
male children that were in Bethlehem, and in all the borders
thereof, from two years old and under, according to the time
which he had carefully learned of the wise men. Then was
fulfilled that which was spoken by Jeremiah the prophet, saying,*

> *A voice was heard in Ramah,*
> *Weeping and great mourning,*
> *Rachel weeping for her children;*
> *And she would not be comforted,*
> *because they are not.*

*But when Herod was dead, behold, an angel of the Lord
appeareth in a dream to Joseph in Egypt, saying, Arise and take
the young child and his mother, and go into the land of Israel:
for they are dead that sought the young child's life. And he
arose and took the young child and his mother, and came into
the land of Israel. But when he heard that Archelaus was
reigning over Judaea in the room of his father Herod, he was
afraid to go thither; and being warned of God in a dream, he
withdrew into the parts of Galilee, and came and dwelt in a city
called Nazareth: that it might be fulfilled which was spoken by
the prophets, that he should be called a Nazarene.*

36

DURING the early years of Christian history, there was a
story in circulation of Jewish origin which alleged that Jesus
had once lived in Egypt. The Talmud says: "Ten measures
of sorcery descended into the world; Egypt received nine,
the rest of the world one." I know some people who wouldn't
find that difficult to believe now! But the story was meant to
discredit Jesus. *He* had lived in Egypt; he went there,
according to the story, because he was illegitimate, and in
Egypt he worked as a labourer. Being intelligent, he learned
magic, returned to Palestine with the formulae tatooed on his
skin, and thus was able to perform miracles. . . .

Now, what would *you* do if some scandalous story were
being circulated about someone you admired? Some story
which you knew perfectly well had some grain of factual
truth in it, but had become so hopelessly distorted as now to
be almost wholly untrue? What would you do? Wouldn't
you try to circulate the true account? And that is precisely
what St. Matthew attempted to do in the second half of the
second chapter of his gospel. He attempted to tell the *truth*
about the sojourn-in-Egypt rumour. So that chapter 2, like
chapter 1, of his book is half apology.

What is the truth about the connection of Jesus with
Egypt? St. Matthew says he was taken there as a baby! and
that is all there is to it. He returned while still a baby. Of
course, imagination has got busy on this. In the old Coptic
quarter of Cairo is a crypt where the Holy family is supposed
to have stayed, and a sycamore tree under which Mary is
supposed to have loved to sit. But we don't really know anything concerning Jesus in Egypt except why he went. And
this St. Matthew explains in order to stifle rumours. Not that
he did altogether: we find them resurrected by Celsus in the
third century.

But this is what St. Matthew tells us. Herod, the half-Jew
king of Judea, realised that the Magi had fooled him by not

disclosing the whereabouts of the child they had come to honour. So he resolved upon the slaughter of *all* the children in Bethlehem to make sure of no risks to his throne. Joseph sensed this might happen; or, as St. Matthew puts it, the Lord spoke to him in a dream: "Arise and take the young child and his mother, and flee into Egypt, and be thou there until I tell thee: for Herod will seek the young child to destroy him."

Herod *did* seek the young child to destroy him; and all the children in Bethlehem of two years and under perished in consequence—perhaps thirty babies, not more. Joseph would expect trouble of a king of Herod's stamp, who was so jealous that he strangled one of his own sons with his own hands, had his lovely wife Mariamne murdered, and arranged the death of notable men of Jerusalem at his funeral so as to be sure there were some genuine tears shed on the occasion. Joseph would only sleep in fits and starts while Herod reigned after the Magi had visited his humble home.

And so you see the little family on the coast road making for Egypt, a pathetic sight. In all this narrative Joseph, I notice, dominates the scene, not Mary. It is the most we hear of him. Poor Joseph! We never see him but he is in trouble. Shall he marry Mary? Where can he find accommodation where she can have her child? Must they flee by the road to Egypt? And twelve years later, had they lost the boy on the visit to Jerusalem? After which we hear no more of Joseph. But he was a good father. And he was a good husband. You could tell that if you saw that donkey on the Egypt road, with Mary on its back, a child in her arms, and Joseph walking with watchful eyes, watching for robbers.

Tradition says robbers did appear. They saw that bundle. It might be gold. They made a grab at it. But seeing the child and seeing the mother's face, they left them both alone. And the next time Jesus met that robber was on the Cross on Calvary's mount—the penitent thief. True? I do not know. But that is how it was on the Egypt road. And if you are a Christian, and if you believe what I believe, you have to get your mind round to the idea of God on that donkey beset with thieves!

I shall touch on that thought in a minute's time. But first let me be critical. *Did* Jesus go down into Egypt? Was St. Matthew perhaps conjuring up the idea so as to make Jesus' history seem parallel with Israel's: "Out of Egypt did I call my son." The narrative does borrow phrases from Moses. But I do not think this means invention. And for this reason, that St. Matthew's quotations from the Old Testament are singularly inappropriate unless read into by an actual event, including the quotation from Jeremiah.

How long were they in Egypt? A year perhaps? Two years? Then when Herod the Great was dead, Joseph took "the young child and his mother" (such is the repeated phrase in this piece of narrative) back to Palestine and then to Nazareth as a safer place, Archelaus a tyrant occupying Judea's throne.

* * *

I have called my sermon this morning "guarding the King". That is what Joseph did. That is what Mary did. They took care of Christ. And it is all so illuminating because if men had invented the story, they would have had a miraculous intervention to take care of Christ. An angel would have carried him on angel wings to safety in Egypt. But God does not use miracles when ordinary means suffice. And God does not contract out of risk. So we must not expect God to lift *us* out of the hazards of life but to protect us through them. And we must take the precautions of wisdom; and make use of such ordinary means for our welfare as life provides— medicine, fresh air, recreation. Religion must never be a substitute for common sense. We must take care of ourselves.

All this in passing. What I wish to emphasise, and what I think the narrative teaches, is that, while it is true that Christ is our Saviour, there is a sense in which we must take care of him. This Joseph did on the road to Egypt and in the little town of Nazareth whither they returned. And this the Church must do. It must take care of Christ. It must do it because it can lose Christ. It can lose sight of Christ. It can become obsessed with ritual and order and history. And then it fails to be much of a means of grace. It can also lose its contact with the historic events of the gospel and degenerate into a philosophy of religion or a humanitarian ethic. After which it has no reason for existence. And it is on this count that some find the doctrine of an Apostolic succession in the Church attractive. Not as an automatic means of grace; but if the ministry is actually traceable back through the Bishops to the Apostles themselves, there is a valuable contact here with historic Christianity not lightly to be thrown away.

"Herod will seek the young child to destroy him." That was the case and still is the case. And if you stumble at the thought of the Church needing to take care of Christ, it is no more remarkable than Joseph doing precisely the same on the road to Egypt. Oh, I know about the humility of it all. I know about the seeming incongruity of it all. The eternal fleeing on a donkey! It is the scandal of particularity "writ large". But when we accept this historic event, we shall not expect Christianity to flourish without the Church. We shall not fall into the trap of saying we will have the Christ but not the Church. The Church takes care of Christ.

"Herod will seek the young child to destroy him." Herod is with us still. He is looking for the child in *your* arms. Herod's other names are Humanism, Rationalism and militant Secularism. He will explain your faith away, or laugh your faith away, or entice your faith away. My friend, if you are a Christian, you will have to take care of Christ in your life. It means giving your mind to your faith. It means giving discipline to your church-going, and a watch on your practice. "Herod will seek the young child to destroy him."

All this calls for watchfulness, application and resolve. But the young child *was* taken care of, even by Joseph with a donkey on the open road to Egypt. Herod was fooled. And he will be fooled again if the Church means business, and you and I mean business. We shall keep our faith, that precious bundle, which comes to be our Saviour. We shall keep it unto life eternal.

4. THE KING'S TEMPTATION

St. Matthew, Chapter 4, vv. 1-11

Then was Jesus led up of the Spirit into the wilderness to be tempted of the devil. And when he had fasted forty days and forty nights, he afterward hungered. And the tempter came and said unto him, If thou art the Son of God, command that these stones become bread. But he answered and said, It is written, Man shall not live by bread alone, but by every word that proceedeth out of the mouth of God. Then the devil taketh him into the holy city; and he set him on the pinnacle of the temple, and saith unto him, If thou art the Son of God, cast thyself down: for it is written,

> *He shall give his angels charge concerning thee:*
> *And on their hands they shall bear thee up,*
> *Lest haply thou dash thy foot against a stone.*

Jesus said unto him, Again it is written, Thou shalt not tempt the Lord thy God. Again, the devil taketh him unto an exceeding high mountain, and sheweth him all the kingdoms of the world, and the glory of them; and he said unto him, All these things will I give thee, if thou wilt fall down and worship me. Then saith Jesus unto him, Get thee hence, Satan: for it is written, Thou shalt worship the Lord thy God, and him only shalt thou serve. Then the devil leaveth him; and behold, angels came and ministered unto him.

MATTHEW 4, v. 1: Then was Jesus led up of the Spirit into the wilderness to be tempted of the devil.

THAT'S an extraordinary thing! Indeed the whole narrative is full of extraordinary things! It is an extraordinary thing that a wilderness should be a place of temptations. You could understand it if some young man came up to Piccadilly and was tempted of the devil. Or he began work in some business enterprise where "sharp practices" were entertained and there he was tempted of the devil. Or some girl along with many other girls in one of the Services got tempted of the devil. But Jesus was tempted in the *wilderness*!

Do you know what the Judean wilderness was like? It was like some huge crucible among the mountains wherein some superhuman power had conducted some fantastic experiment. And there was nothing left but a tortuous mass of twisted rock and cinder: no blade of grass to relieve the slatey greyness, no tree, no living thing save an occasional jackal howling. In that *emptiness* Jesus was tempted.

Did you know you can be tempted in emptiness? Sometimes we imagine that if all the Piccadillys, gambling dens and get-rich-quick rackets were suppressed no man would ever be tempted again. But temptation has everything to do with the kingdom of the mind, so that even if you or I find ourselves in empty places we take our minds with us. Jesus was tempted in the *wilderness*!

Perhaps we are surprised that Jesus should be tempted at all! But he was! And not only once, but throughout his ministry. Indeed the temptation narrative may be a pictorial representation by Jesus of his own intermittent psychological experience for months, if not years on end! It has to do with power. Most often temptation has to do with power. More particularly with what a man knows of his own powers. Here's a man with unusual power of leadership. He will be tempted to browbeat. Here is a girl with great power over the other sex; she will be tempted to entangle. Temptation has everything to do with the usage of your own powers.

And Jesus had power. This temptation narrative is set in juxtaposition to the baptism narrative, not necessarily because they happened together, but because whenever Jesus heard the voice of God in his own soul "Thou art my beloved Son", immediately he heard the voice of the tempter urging him to use his power for wrongful ends.

Look at the temptation narrative . . . there is a psychological arrangement. First, Jesus was tempted to doubt—"If thou be the Son of God." Secondly, he was tempted to test—"If thou be the Son of God, cast thyself down from hence." Thirdly, he was tempted to use his powers to *snatch* at Kingship—"All these things will I give thee," says the Devil, "if thou will fall down and worship me." It was a temptation to quick results the wrong way. A temptation to bring in the Kingdom by easier means than by living with people and suffering with people and dying for people. And stunts and portents are the means that suggest themselves to the mind. But Jesus rejected them. They may draw crowds, but they do not bring faith. They may look startling, but they do not prove divinity.

Yes, there is something about all this that was peculiar to Jesus. But every Vicar knows something of its essence. And every Church knows something. And every Parochial Church Council, and every man in the pew keen to see his congregation grow. It is a temptation to pack the Church *quickly*.

And what forms does the temptation take? The three, I think, set out in this temptation narrative. First, to turn stones into bread. To seek to spend time primarily in supplying the material needs of people. To go over, perhaps, to some political programme for social amelioration. And let there be no misunderstanding. We *must* concern ourselves with men's bodies as well as their souls. We are not to be narrowly parochial, wrapped up in a religious world all our own. The refugee problem is our concern. Education is our concern. Housing is our concern. But none of these is to be sought after as a method for filling our churches. They will not produce faith.

Secondly, there is the temptation to stunts. It *is* a temptation to succumb to the idea that television broadcasts can do the trick, or sound radio can do the trick, or adventurous

43

musical programmes can do the trick. And people will be queueing up to enter the church's doors! And mark you, all of these devices must not be rejected by the Church. But there is no *trick* by which people can be brought to God's kingdom; men cannot be tricked there, only *won* there—and the means are work and patience and friendship.

And then thirdly, there are the devil's tools. Whole Churches have fallen into this trap. A man must say what he thinks! I believe the political Churches use these tools. You can see their use in Europe. You could see it in Cyprus. I know the result may be packed-out churches, but it is a way Jesus turned against. It constituted the third temptation. But he resisted it.

> The kingdom, that I seek
> Is Thine; so let the way
> That leads to it be Thine,
> Else I must surely stray.
>
> (H. Bonar.)

And what course did he follow instead? He followed the course of beginning quietly. He personally attracted a few men, he taught those few men. He did not, as it were, stand in some church porch leaning out to sweep men in; he went down with them where they were, into their boats, into their market places, into their lives, yes, and into their sufferings, so far into their sufferings that he tasted death for every man. Jesus' method was to redeem by personal friendship, a slow and costly process. And on every "flashy" way he steadfastly turned his back.

* * *

Am I addressing someone with temptations this morning? Am I addressing anyone *without* temptations? I put it like this because even if you are as good as Jesus you will still be tempted. God's royalty was tempted. I don't of course know your temptations. In any case they will be different from mine. Temptations vary because powers vary; and temptation is always related to power. There are temptations to pride, sensuality and cynicism even in the most unexpected people.

44

And some are tempted to doubt the existence of the life to come. . . .

But there are lessons here to deal with them. The first is to tackle them in the mind in solitude, that is, in the wilderness; to tackle them before they issue in any kind of action. All of which means that it does matter what a man thinks, and what he sees, and what he reads. Temptation to be defeated in the act must first of all be defeated in the mind. So that if we let ourselves think what we will, we shall find ourselves on the wrong foot, or on no feet at all, when the enemy comes in like a flood. As a man thinks, so is he, which is why St. Paul wrote, "Whatsoever things are true, lovely and of good repute, *think* on these things."

And the second lesson is this. It is derived from the fact that Jesus resisted the Tempter by quotation from scripture —"*It is written*, man shall not live by bread alone." "*It is written*, thou shalt not tempt the Lord thy God." "*It is written*, thou shalt worship the Lord thy God and Him only shalt thou serve." We shall never defeat our temptations if we live without a fixed standard. It is useless charging into battle if you do not know what you are fighting for. And the most perilous position is to question the Christian standards when the fight is on—the Christian standards about marriage, adultery, and other men's goods; the Church's doctrine about the life beyond this life. The only way to victory is to say, "Here I stand, for it is written."

Of course we fall. Often we fall. Sexagesima Sunday (which to-day is) reminds us of the fall of man. But there is God's forgiveness to be had. And it is a much more Christian attitude to own that we fall and seek that forgiveness than to try to tamper with the standards.

And all the way through there are the resources of God's grace. They come to us through Christ. For he did not only conquer in his temptation to show us what to do, he conquered to make his strength available. Or as the writer of the Epistle to the Hebrews puts it: "For we have not a high priest that cannot be touched with the feeling of our infirmities; but one that hath been in all points tempted like as we are, yet without sin. Let us therefore draw near with boldness unto the throne of grace, that we may find grace to help us in time of need."

So let us tackle our temptations in the kingdom of the mind. Let us be sure we have our standards fixed. And when the day of temptation comes, as surely it *will* come, let us run to Christ for his assistance, for he can meet our need.

5. THE KING AND THE LAW

St. Matthew, Chapter 5, vv. 17-20

Think not that I came to destroy the law or the prophets: I came not to destroy, but to fulfil. For verily I say unto you, Till heaven and earth pass away, one jot or one tittle shall in no wise pass away from the law, till all things be accomplished.

Whosoever therefore shall break one of these least commandments, and shall teach men so, shall be called least in the kingdom of heaven: but whosoever shall do and teach them, he shall be called great in the kingdom of heaven.

For I say unto you, that except your righteousness shall exceed the righteousness of the scribes and Pharisees, ye shall in no wise enter into the kingdom of heaven.

MATTHEW 5, v. 17: Think not that I came to destroy the law or the prophets: I came not to destroy, but to fulfil.

I WONDER if you've ever been misunderstood? I wonder if you've tried hard to make yourself plain, and your hearers have derived the wrong impression? I have. It has happened to me many times. It has happened over preaching. It has happened over broadcasting. You take endless trouble with sentences, turning them this way and that, hoping you cannot possibly be misunderstood, but you are misunderstood. You can tell it by the letters people write, one or two extremely rude.

It is, in a way then, comforting to realise that Jesus was misunderstood. On two occasions at least this happened. People were beginning to think that he implied complete absence of conflict everywhere as a result of his coming. And

47

it isn't true. So he had to say: "Think not that I came to sow peace on the earth. I come not to sow peace but a sword." And the saying is so hard, it must be authentic, no one would have invented this.

And then people began wondering if Jesus was opposed to the religious rules and regulations of his day. I don't wonder they thought this. After all, he did heal men on the Sabbath, and in Jewish praxis you were not supposed to heal men on the Sabbath. And when he was invited out to a meal (as he often was), he deliberately omitted to go through the motions of ritual washing which the law required. And when his disciples plucked ears of corn and rubbed them between their hands to separate out the grain to eat them, he justified the action by reference to David's eating of "the shew-bread", thereby demonstrating the precedence of human need over law. Jesus in fact seemed to treat the law in his own way, even to be above it. One day he touched a leper to heal him, which touching was clean contrary to law, and then followed this by bidding the cleansed man offer his gift of thanksgiving as the law required! I don't wonder the people were puzzled.

So Jesus had to tell them: "Think not that I came to destroy the law or the prophets: I came not to destroy, but to fulfil."

What was he destroying? He was destroying the accretions to the Mosaic law which had made the whole corpus fantastic. As things came to stand in Jewry, a man musn't even write on the Sabbath, at least not two letters of the alphabet in juxtaposition, though he could write one on one wall and another on another! And he couldn't apply wadding smeared with ointment to a wound on the Sabbath, though he could apply the wadding *without* the ointment. Nor could his wife wear a brooch on her dress, or an ornamental pin, on the Sabbath, it would be equivalent to carrying a burden. What was worse, in later times, an orthodox Jew couldn't wear false teeth on the Sabbath! It would be carrying a burden! All this is what Jesus undercut. And do you wonder! He saw many a Jew abandon his religion entirely, so completely unreasonable did it seem; which indeed has happened with many Jews to-day. And the whole fault lay in the fact that the general principles of the Mosaic law had been read as if they were rules; and therefore exceptions had to be tabulated, and more and more exceptions, till the whole body of rules and exceptions developed into what was called "the tradition of the elders", or the oral law; and this in the third century was embodied in the Mishnah, and, later still, in the Babylonian and Jerusalem Talmuds running into many volumes to explain the Mishnah. All this legal approach to religion Jesus completely undercut by his actions, as if he were a king, king of law.

*　　*　　*

What was Jesus destroying? Once more we ask the question. He was destroying that attitude to law which merely tries to fulfil it in the letter, to the complete ignoring of the underlying spirit. Judaism was riddled with this. A Jew wouldn't light a fire on the Sabbath; but that was very inconvenient, so he hired Gentiles to do it for him! And we tend to smile and pity the Jews for being very foolish. But all religions tend to become legalistic. Even the Christian religion tends to become legalistic. It wasn't for nothing Luther headed a Reformation. If Christians think they can laugh at unreasonableness in the synagogue, Jews can laugh back at unreasonableness in the Church. The blunt fact is, when any religions move away from ministering *principles* of conduct and not rules, and so omit to leave individuals to work them out for themselves in their own situation, legalism results; and the end of legalism is fiddling, dodging and casuistry, in fact the lowering of moral standards instead of raising them.

Some of you will remember what happened to civilian life during the last war. We had laws, so many laws governing every aspect of our lives a man could scarcely live without transgressing some. And the result was dodging of the law, dodging till it became normal to dodge. And when that happens, the moral standard has begun to rot from underneath. It may partly account for the declining standards which obtain to-day.

*　　*　　*

49

What was Jesus destroying by his regal attitude towards the Jewish law? A third time we ask the question. And the answer is, he was destroying all hope of law as a method to obtain the standards of the law.

You will note he was not abolishing law. He was not denying the necessity of standards. He was not implying Christian standards are lower than the Jewish. He went so far as to assert that one jot or one tittle should in no wise pass away from the law, that is to say, not even the smallest letter in the law, or even part of a letter, could be abolished. And as if this were not emphasis enough, he said that except Christian disciples reached a higher standard than that of the Scribes and Pharisees they simply would not enter the Kingdom of Heaven!

Let us be absolutely clear on this. The situation is not as one French peasant thought it was when reproved by his priest for committing some specific sin: "Mais, mon père, I thought Christ died for our sins so that we could go on committing them and reach heaven just the same!"

No, Christianity does not abolish laws of morality. It does not wink at fiddling, cheating, prostituting and smuggling. And modern smugglers don't use muffled oars and coves in South Devon, they simply try to dodge Her Majesty's Customs and Excise Authority at the ports! Oh, it is not for nothing the Ten Commandments are embedded even in the Communion Service, the most Christian and spiritual service of all. The spiritual life cannot be lived in independence of moral standards. But what Jesus destroyed is all hope of making people live up to those standards by the presence of law.

And this is very true of us in the Church to-day; while concurring in the need to set in order Church of England canon law, do not expect to see a sudden rise in standards as a consequence. Law is necessary, but law as a method to uphold law is very weak indeed.

* * *

This brings me to my final point. How then did Jesus

fulfil the law? How does the Church in so far as it is true to Christ fulfil it to-day? The answer is—by attention to the spirit of the law as well as to its letter. This is why, in the Sermon on the Mount (from which my text for this morning is taken), you will find Jesus stressing motives underlying acts. So hate is equivalent to murder, and the lustful eye is equivalent to adultery.

But there is even more than this. Jesus fulfilled the law by bringing in the person of himself as the incentive to keep it. The truth is, love of a person will get us all to do what no amount of rules and regulations could ever hope to accomplish. For love, people will go to the ends of the earth and even throw their lives away. So Jesus brought the way of love as incentive in religion. God's love of us, our love for God; "God so loved the world that he gave his only begotten Son." That is the basis of all real religion which lifts us up to higher standards. Not just a command, but a statement! Not just a prohibition, but an offer! This is the royal way by which law is kept. And when you hear this way adopted in any Christian Church, you hear then the authentic ring of Christianity. Not law first, but love first and then the law is far more likely to be kept. This was ever Jesus' way. I hope we keep it here. I hope you hear from this pulpit always the authentic ring of Christian preaching.

6. THE KING'S TOUCH

ST. MATTHEW, CHAPTER 9, VV. 18-31

While he spake these things unto them, behold, there came a ruler, and worshipped him, saying, My daughter is even now dead: but come and lay thy hand upon her, and she shall live. And Jesus arose, and followed him, and so did his disciples.

And behold, a woman, who had an issue of blood twelve years, came behind him, and touched the border of his garment, for she said within herself, If I do but touch his garment, I shall be made whole. But Jesus turning and seeing her said, Daughter, be of good cheer; thy faith hath made thee whole. And the woman was made whole from that hour.

And when Jesus came into the ruler's house and saw the flute-players, and the crowd making a tumult, he said, Give place: for the damsel is not dead, but sleepeth. And they laughed him to scorn. But when the crowd was put forth, he entered in, and took her by the hand; and the damsel arose. And the fame hereof went forth into all that land.

And as Jesus passed by from thence, two blind men followed him, crying out, and saying, Have mercy on us, thou son of David. And when he was come into the house, the blind men came to him: and Jesus saith unto them, Believe ye that I am able to do this? They say unto him, Yea, Lord. Then touched he their eyes saying, According to your faith be it done unto you. And their eyes were opened. And Jesus strictly charged them, saying, See that no man know it. But they went forth, and spread abroad his fame in all that land.

MATTHEW 9, v. 18: My daughter is even now dead: but come and lay thy hand upon her, and she shall live.

ON a stretch of desolate marshland in East Anglia there used to stand a strange tarred wooden summer-house. There was no other building for half a mile, and then only a herdsman's house and a mill for pumping water from the dykes up into the river. But from time to time, even in the depths of winter, with the marshbirds wheeling in the wind and screeching overhead, there could have been seen an old but energetic man walking with a fourteen-year-old boy making for that shanty. Clearly the boy was thrilled by the old man, and not surprisingly—a former Welsh rugger captain, a scratch golfer, no mean cricketer at Cambridge and with only half a hand, the rest was shot away. (What a story, and how he told it!) Trained for the Law, then ordained; he was a man of courtly manners, beautiful voice, an excellent preacher with unusual knowledge of the scriptures. And could you have crept over that marsh at night to peer into the windows, you would have seen them both together, the old man and the boy, a large Bible and a Greek Testament between them under the lamplight, hour after hour, reading, questioning, answering till the boy almost cried in desperation or fell asleep in weariness.

And now the years have rolled away, the winds still sweep over the marshland, but the shanty is no more and the clergyman is dead; but the boy still lives with unforgettable memories of that master touch, it made him and inspired him. And I know the story is true for it is of myself, a Vicar now in Kensington.

The master touch upon another life! The king's touch! The touch of Christ. Is there anything more influential? St. Matthew didn't think there was. And so with words he paints us pictures, Impressionist pictures, pictures without details, pictures quite unlike St. Mark's, sometimes even copied from St. Mark, leaving out the details, but pictures that leave the strong impression that Jesus' touch was masterly— it brought *life*, it brought *health*, it brought the *power to see*. . . .

Let us look at those pictures. They hang together in the ninth chapter of St. Matthew. First there is a picture of a

53

crowded room. It is an unattractive crowd, dull clothes, torn clothes, strained faces; and in the corner flute-players wallowing in weird fantastic ululations. And all because within another room a child was lying dead—or so they thought. St. Matthew does not give us names, he only vaguely calls the father of the child "a ruler"—but impressionists in painting do not give you details, only an idea, and here it is the Christ entering, the King of Life entering the room of death, and with his master touch—yes, only with the action of his hand—he brings that child to life.

You can go on discussing if you like for many hours whether or not that child was really dead. You can, if you like, with modern readers, take our Lord's words as they stand: "She is not dead but sleepeth"; and the Greek is partly on your side. And yet St. Luke in his recording seems to count the child as dead—or why did he write "And her spirit returned"? St. Luke, as a doctor, would write with care.

What is the answer to this question? I have to say I do not know—but this I know for very surety: St. Matthew cries aloud to tell us "Christ's was the master touch". Men might wail, women might weep, all hope of life in any fullness might long be left behind—but when Christ touches with his touch, everything is changed. You never know what possibilities exist till he has entered in.

I have seen this happen. I can think now of a face, a woman's face—hard, disillusioned, cynical, such a face as perhaps you only see in cities such as London. Who ever would have dreamt of seeing her worshipping on Sundays. But she does worship, every week. 'Tis true, you can scarcely recognise her. All the deadness has gone out of her face, the harshness and hostility. Why? I know no other explanation—Christ has touched her life. . . .

And we look to see another picture. Once again impressionist. No details. No comprehension. Quite unlike St. Mark. Instead the impression of a swarming crowd. They shove. They smell. And squeezing through—a woman. Strained face. Nervous eyes. Work-worn hands. She carries no ashes of an ostrich's egg in a cotton bag to heal her of her plague.

She carries no barley corn found in the dung of a white she-ass. She has long since given up all hope of those fantastic Jewish remedies. And now, breaking the rule never to mix in any crowd lest she pollute them, she squeezes in, touching men to right and left. What for? Only to touch a tassel you could see to-day on any Jewish praying shawl. But this tassel belonged to Jesus. And she did touch it. And for the moment time stood still. Jesus addressed her—an excommunicated, superstitious, ailing woman. "Daughter!"—what music! "Daughter, thy faith hath made thee whole." And she *was* made whole, simply by the touch of Christ, the king's touch, the masterly touch.

I do not think we need doubt the historicity of this story. If in Harley Street to-day doctors cure by the touch of their hands and the words of their lips, why not Jesus years ago? After all, his was the stronger personality. And now we know how body and mind affect each other. But do we? If we do, we ought to believe St. Matthew's picture when it says that the touch of Christ upon your life will turn you into another person. You will feel better, feel better physically. What you believe in your heart affects the way your body functions. And if you believe in a Father God, watching and providing, a renewing peace can touch your nerves.

* * *

But still there is another picture. This time not abbreviation of material which St. Mark provides, but a story by St. Matthew all his own, or perhaps even duplicating a story of his own. Two men, blind men, men with arms outstretched groping their way into a house. And as they grope, they cry to Jesus, "Have mercy on us thou son of David."

And who are these men? It could be you. It could be me. It could be our whole generation before it finds its way to Christ. In some way it is the common disease of England now. Spiritual blindness caused in no small measure by the triviality engendered by the popular Press. The preoccupation with obtaining money by "lucky breaks", the sheer secularity of outlook on life, battering at the doors of almost everyone

55

—and once these guests are entertained, spiritual blindness is the inevitable result. And then we could be mirrored in St. Matthew's picture, blind men, groping, shuffling, stumbling. . . .

And what is the answer? St. Matthew says—the touch of Christ upon our eyes. And yet we have to grope our way to him to show that we mean business. But then he touches with his touch, the king's touch, the masterly touch. And then the eyes are opened.

Is it fanciful to draw attention to the fact that the first sight these opened eyes perceived was the face of Christ? But I do not think our religion is a personal force unless we too have seen. Ceremony there must be. Liturgy there must be. Canon Law and Convocations. But unless we each have seen the eyes of Christ looking at ourselves we have not reached the centre of religion.

* * *

Come back to these three pictures hanging side by side in St. Matthew, chapter 9. Undoubtedly it is the purpose of this Gospel to lead us to the Saviour's teaching. His teaching is reported. His teaching is collected into groups within the confines of this book. But what is teaching without the teacher? And what is the teacher without a master touch? So St. Matthew also gives us pictures. We see Christ touching here and there and always bringing life and healing. And as we leave these pictures, this is what we ask—Is the touch of Christ upon my life, the King's touch, the masterly touch? I can have it if I will. And what would others say of me? Those who know me, those who meet me—Have I in any sense a master touch? What difference do *I* make to other people? . . .

7. THE KING'S ENEMIES

St. Matthew, Chapter 16, vv. 1-12

And the Pharisees and Sadducees came, and tempting him asked him to shew them a sign from heaven. But he answered and said unto them, When it is evening, ye say, It will be fair weather: for the heaven is red. And in the morning, It will be foul weather to-day: for the heaven is red and lowering. Ye know how to discern the face of the heaven; but ye cannot discern the signs of the times. An evil and adulterous generation seeketh after a sign; and there shall no sign be given unto it, but the sign of Jonah. And he left them, and departed.

And the disciples came to the other side and forgot to take bread. And Jesus said unto them, Take heed and beware of the leaven of the Pharisees and Sadducees. And they reasoned among themselves, saying, We took no bread. And Jesus perceiving it said, O ye of little faith, why reason ye among yourselves, because ye have no bread? Do ye not perceive, neither remember the five loaves of the five thousand, and how many baskets ye took up? Neither the seven loaves of the four thousand, and how many baskets ye took up? How is it that ye do not perceive that I spake not to you concerning bread? But beware of the leaven of the Pharisees and Sadducees. Then understood they how that he bade them not beware of the leaven of bread, but of the teaching of the Pharisees and Sadducees.

MATTHEW 16, v. 6: Take heed and beware of
the leaven of the Pharisees and Sadducees.

I WONDER if you have any enemies; personal enemies, I mean, people who are "up against you"? I wonder if I have? Perhaps you think a Christian oughtn't to have enemies, and certainly a clergyman oughtn't to have enemies! But I have to remind you this morning that *Jesus* had enemies. Not that he wanted to have them. Not that he didn't try to turn them into friends. But when they wouldn't turn they were in fact his enemies. Pharisees and Sadducees, such were their names.

Who were these people who must be counted as enemies of Jesus?

Take first the Pharisees. They possessed a brilliant history. They were the successors of those zealous reformers who, under Ezra and Nehemiah, reconstituted Jewish life when the remnants of their nation found themselves once more encamped on Jewish soil, their exile in the background.

The word "Pharisees" means "separatists". It means that in the century before our Lord these were the Puritan party in this Jewish Church. They were seen as Puritans because, while willing to assist Judaeus Maccabaeus in resisting the denationalising policy of Greece in the year 167 B.C., they *separated* themselves when in the year 135 B.C. the Maccabaean rulers wished to press on and fight for *civil* liberty. These separatists, Hasidim, "pious ones" or Pharisees as they came to be called, were only interested in religion, and in this they differed widely from the Sadducees.

There were some six or seven thousand Pharisees in the time of our Lord who were actually members of the party (so to speak), though there were many followers. On initiation they took two vows: one, to tithe everything eaten, bought or sold; the other, never to be the guest of the nation's common people. Not that they were aristocrats, those were the Sadducees. The Pharisees stood for the people *against* the Sadducees, but the people needed to be taught, and they were the ones to teach them. In Jesus' time they were at the height of their power, and because they wielded power they were half-feared, half-hated by the people generally. They have been compared with the Jesuits in the Roman Catholic Church.

Over against the Pharisees or Puritans there were the Sadducees. These, too, were back from exile with "the pious ones", but these were the court party, the priestly court party, the party with Zerubbabel. So they grew to be the snobbish party in the Holy Land. To them belonged the priests, in particular, the High Priests, and in more particular still, Caiaphas, the High Priest who conducted Jesus' trial. Their religion centred on the Temple and they were very rich. The Pharisees' religion centred on the synagogues, and they eyed each other from afar with evident distrust. Especially as in the days we read of in the gospels the synagogues were gaining ground in influence. And so to counteract this, the Sadducees manipulated political strings of power, politics and religion closely interwoven.

* * *

And someone in the congregation is growing weary of all this. You can't follow this intrigue and political corruption. And I half want you to grow weary of it. Then you cannot rest content and think the life of faith in God an easy thing in Palestine when Jesus lived. It was anything but easy. Judea and Galilee were riddled with every form of religious trickery, snobbery, class hatred, and downright hypocrisy which the mind of man can possibly conceive. Everyone went in fear and trembling of putting a foot wrong. Everyone thought twice before he dared reveal his thoughts, lest he find his neighbour a member of the opposite gang. And there were spies to contend with, and informers to beware of. You never knew when you might be dragged before the courts or excommunicated from the synagogue, and then you might as well be dead, for very few dared trade with you.

Have you any enemies? Had Jesus any enemies? Yes, he had these Pharisees and Sadducees. And the day came when he spoke up plain and clear to his disciples: "Beware of the leaven of the Pharisees and Sadducees." And so dull of imagination were these men and so preoccupied with having forgotten to buy bread that they thought Jesus, too, was occupied with bread. It was the word "leaven" they had fastened on. But Jesus was referring to the teaching of the Pharisees and Sadducees. It *works* like leaven, that is to say,

59

although a tiny portion only is inserted in any baking of the daily bread, nevertheless it works and works, penetrating the whole, making it other than it was.

And the teaching of the Pharisees and Sadducees was like that. And you give me your *deaf* ear because you imagine all these men are now extinct. But I tell you, wherever religion walks, these men walk. And as they were enemies of Jesus in his day, so they are inimical to spiritual religion in this our day.

* * *

What is the leaven of the Pharisees? It is separatism. It is the idea that true religion is something which can be taught, learned, and then practised. You pick up the customs, you pick up the language, then you repeat them, after which you will pass with all those others who are initiated into the same circle. They are pious? Yes. Good in their way? Yes. You will find them in the Low Church, and you will find them in the High Church. In the main you will always find them at the extremes, which is why extremes so often meet. Remember it is not first a party, it is a way of looking at religion. It is separatism, separatism from all who do not go their way. And Jesus said "Beware of it"—because it makes for terrifying pride, terrifying because it hinders spiritual religion.

And then the leaven of the Sadducees. And what is that? A look at their doctrines will tell you. They believed neither in angels, nor in spirits, nor in a resurrection after death. So it is not to be wondered at that after Easter *they* were the enemies of the Christian Church. But what is the spirit of Saduceeism? One word will tell you—Rationalism. We must beware of it. It is an enemy of Christ.

I have been called a Rationalist! By some I have been cold-shouldered as a Rationalist, but such is all misunderstanding. By Rationalism I do not mean applying reason to religion. Would to God that more of it were applied. It would clear out some of the lumber. It would clear out some of the super-stition. No, a Rationalist is one who cannot find the room in all his view of life for any kind of supernatural. And it's a

60

spirit. It can get inside you and it can get inside me—I pray, but I doubt if it will really make any difference. I come to church not because I'm sure there is a God at all but because religion is the safeguard of our public morals. Don't you see the point? Religion for expediency's sake. That is Sadducee-ism. And at the risk of being misunderstood, let me add this point—when Christianity is supported because it is a bulwark against the Communist threat, that is Sadduceeism. Religion sought for political ends. And once that leaven starts to work within a Church, there will not be much standing ground for spiritual religion.

* * *

The Pharisees and the Sadducees! How they hated each other, but they united once to entangle Jesus by asking him a sign from heaven. It is the context of my verse to-day: "Beware of the leaven of the Pharisees and Sadducees." And they united again to bring him to the Cross. For however much they hated each other, they hated Jesus more than all. It is because Christ stands for the downfall of Separatism in religion and Rationalism in religion. And if we would find ourselves at one with him, we, too, must beware of the leaven of the Pharisees and Sadducees. They are the King's enemies.

8. WHEN THE KING REFUSES

St. Matthew, Chapter 20, vv. 17-28

And as Jesus was going up to Jerusalem, he took the twelve disciples apart, and in the way he said unto them, Behold, we go up to Jerusalem; and the Son of Man shall be delivered unto the chief priests and scribes; and they shall condemn him to death, and shall deliver him unto the Gentiles to mock, and to scourge, and to crucify: and the third day he shall be raised up.

Then came to him the mother of the sons of Zebedee with her sons, worshipping him, and asking a certain thing of him. And he said unto her, What wouldest thou? She saith unto him, Command that these my two sons may sit, one on thy right hand, and one on thy left hand, in thy Kingdom. But Jesus answered and said, Ye know not what ye ask. Are ye able to drink the cup that I am about to drink? They say unto him, We are able. He saith unto them, My cup indeed ye shall drink: but to sit on my right hand, and on my left hand, is not mine to give, but it is for them for whom it hath been prepared of my Father. And when the ten heard it, they were moved with indignation concerning the two brethren. But Jesus called them unto him, and said, Ye know that the rulers of the Gentiles lord it over them, and their great ones exercise authority over them. Not so shall it be among you: but whosoever would become great among you shall be your minister; and whosoever would be first among you shall be your servant: even as the Son of Man came not to be ministered unto, but to minister, and to give his life a ransom for many.

MATTHEW 20, vv. 21, 22: Command that these my two sons may sit, one on thy right hand, and one on thy left hand, in thy Kingdom. But Jesus answered and said, Ye know not what ye ask.

I WONDER if you've ever been keen on some organisation or good cause, so keen that you thought about it and dreamt about it, and longed to throw your whole weight into it? And then one day you went and offered your services. You never thought of the eventuality that your help wouldn't be wanted. But it wasn't wanted! The promoters of the good cause put it tactfully, but that is what their words amounted to. And you came home crestfallen; and if the truth were known, not a little bitter about life in general. I don't know that there is any experience which hurts more than offering your services and being turned down. And if you think you are the only one to have undergone such an experience, I bring to your notice a scripture passage which reminds us that two Apostles underwent it, two of Christ's chief Apostles, James and John. . . .

May I remind you of the facts? According to St. Matthew, the mother of the sons of Zebedee, that is Salome, came asking for chief places for her two sons in Christ's Kingdom. Perhaps they got their mother to make this request on their behalf. After all, she was the sister of Jesus' mother and she did help the Apostolic band. But whatever the reason, I used to despise James and John for this. I used to count them the fathers of all those ecclesiastical "place-seekers" whom I despise. But I have changed my mind. Not about place-seeking in the Church, but about James and John. What I think they wanted was not a comfortable seat but a spectacular piece of service. They wanted to burn themselves out. They wanted a task of outstanding size. After all, they were men of action. They had energy and to spare. They longed to call down fire from heaven and sweep in the Kingdom of God. And what had they been offered? Following Jesus around villages! Watching him heal the sick! Witnessing his restoration of the weak-willed! "O Master," they cried in effect, "let us *do* something for thee." "O mother Salome, you bid Jesus let us do something for him." And so she goes, not without maternal pride, I think, "Grant that these my two

63

sons may sit, the one on thy right hand and the other on thy left in thy Kingdom."

Now here is a remarkable fact. She wasn't rebuked by Jesus! She did not, as far as we are told, receive any answer at all! I know some commentators suggest the mother didn't ask at all. St. Matthew only put that in out of reverence for James and John; but I doubt it. Anyway, James and John received the answer. Maybe Jesus saw it was a "put-up job". And the answer they received hurt. It hurt terribly. Jesus said, "Ye know not what ye ask." It hurt because they thought they knew very well. But his next words cut deeper still. "Those two places are reserved for others." Doubtless they retired crestfallen. They had offered for heroic service in Christ's Kingdom, and they weren't wanted! Doubtless Salome, their mother, went away crestfallen, too. Her two sons weren't wanted!

Did it ever occur to you, I wonder, that God might not want our service? That's a new view of the sovereignty of God. I cannot say it occurred to me till I considered this scripture. We grow so accustomed to the idea that all the calling to God's service is on God's side and all the refusing is on our side; but the Bible has a knack of turning upside down preconceived notions. Sometimes God does not want our heroic service. Our allegiance? Yes, God always wants that. But quite often nothing startling from us, nothing life-giving, nothing tremendous, only patient following in the routine acts of life; going to the city, working patiently and coming home by the same bus. . . .

I think this is difficult. I think it is far easier to live the heroic life when you are out in the limelight, when people will notice what you say and observe what you do. My heart goes out to James and John. I know how they felt. It is so much easier to live the Christian life when we are called to some big and challenging task. But when we are called to occupy some insignificant platform in life, or scarcely any platform at all; when young people have to stay at home to look after aged parents, when routine jobs occupy so much of our waking hours and we are growing older without seeing the sunny parts

64

of the earth, then it is we grow rebellious against the smallness of our lot. I say I sympathise with James and John, more especially when their offer went unaccepted.

Is this why our Lord wasn't hard on these two men? But the other disciples were. The scripture says "they were moved with indignation". They certainly read the question of James and John as place-seeking. And on that account were given corrective teaching by Jesus. He showed that there have to be leaders in the Christian Church; but there is a difference between leadership there and leadership in the world. In the former, it is a primacy of service. He who is accounted great is he who does most for other people, not he for whom other people do much. In the Church, the supreme leader should be the supreme servant. And if he thoroughly understands this he can seek a chief place. Jesus understood it. He had a chief place, but it meant service unto death, or, as he put it, "Even as the Son of Man came not to be ministered unto, but to minister, and to give his life a ransom for many."

Do I have to remark on that word "ransom"? Only because it has played so large a part in theological theories of the atonement. But do not ask the question to whom the ransom was paid and the phrase will not yield difficulties. Straightforwardly it means Christ's primacy is supreme because he gave his all for our redemption, even his life.

Come back to James and John. Come back to their mother's request: "Command that these my two sons may sit, one on thy right hand, and one on thy left in thy Kingdom." Come back now and look at these men with all the resentment and indignation and envy taken out of your eyes. Learn instead this lesson about unanswered prayer. Salome asked, "Command these places for my sons in thy glory." And Jesus refused. He did not answer that prayer. He said those places were in fact already allotted. He also added, "Ye know not what ye ask." And this is what I am inclined to think, that whenever God does not answer our prayers it is because we do not know what we ask. And here you have it in black and white: "Command that these my two sons may sit, the one on thy right hand and the other on thy left in thy glory" (St. Mark's word). But the day came when, standing by the foot of Christ's Cross, Salome saw what coming in his glory was. It was crucifixion. And to think that she had asked *that* for her two sons! How she must have wanted to tear the tongue out of her mouth! There *was* one on his right hand! and another on his left! Malefactors they were, dying in agony! Oh, if only she had known! But Jesus knew. Therefore he did not grant her request. Perhaps that is why he does not always answer our requests. We do not know what we ask. But God does.

And I am sure some reader has prayed to God with all his heart, "O God, let me out, let me out, I cannot stand this routine another day. I shall scream if I see that wretched office desk again." And God has said "No" to our prayer; and we've had to go back and the routine has had to go on. But we shall be making the mistake of our lives if we are sullen in consequence. We know not what we ask. We may have been asking for crucifixion without knowing it. . . .

Once more we look back at these men. We don't know exactly what happened to John. But we do know what happened to James. With bewildering brevity the end of his life is described in the book of the Acts of the Apostles. "And Herod killed James the brother of John with a sword." Did Salome remember then? Did she remember how Jesus had said, "Ye shall drink of my cup and be baptised with the baptism that I am baptised with." Jesus had been baptised in blood. Did Mary mother of Jesus run to Salome her sister then? "They did it to my son, now they have done it to yours." Did they sit long hours each trying to comfort the other? We do not know. But this we know. James did in the end get what he asked. Perhaps he was ready for it then. And some day for us God may grant our prayer though he denies it now. We shall be ready then. But till then we must be patient, very patient, believing that God knows best what we can manage. . . .

9. WATCHING THE KING

St. Matthew, Chapter 27, vv. 32-44

*And as they came out, they found a man of Cyrene, Simon
by name: him they compelled to go with them, that he might
bear his cross. And when they were come unto a place called
Golgotha, that is to say, The place of a skull, they gave him
wine to drink mingled with gall: and when he had tasted it, he
would not drink. And when they had crucified him, they parted
his garments among them, casting lots: and they sat and watched
him there.*

*And they set up over his head his accusation written, THIS
IS JESUS THE KING OF THE JEWS.*

*Then are there crucified with him two robbers, one on the
right hand, and one on the left. And they that passed by railed
on him, wagging their heads, and saying, Thou that destroyest
the Temple, and buildest it in three days, save thyself: if thou
art the Son of God, come down from the cross. In like manner
also the chief priests mocking him, with the scribes and elders,
said, He saved others; himself he cannot save. He is the King
of Israel; let him now come down from the cross, and we will
believe on him. He trusted on God; let him deliver him now, if
he desireth him: for he said, I am the Son of God.*

*And the robbers also that were crucified with him cast upon
him the same reproach.*

MATTHEW 27, v. 36 (A.V.): And sitting down
they watched him there.

THAT'S what you do when you've finished some task. You
sit down and survey your handiwork. And that's what the
soldiers did at Calvary. They crucified Jesus; they cast lots

for his clothes, and then they sat down to watch him there. That was their Good Friday.

I don't think you ought to be too hard on these men. It was their duty to watch. Twice in the Crucifixion narrative, once at the beginning and once at the end, we are told they watched. They answered with their lives for doing that. They had to see that the crucified died; they had to see that no one came to take him down. In the sense in which all gaolers guard their prisoners, these men guarded Jesus.

I don't know what they saw as they watched. I mean, I don't know what impression was made upon their minds by all that they saw. I don't suppose for one moment they wanted to be there. I don't suppose for one moment they wanted to be in Judea at all, maybe each soldier had a home somewhere in sunny Italy, or a wife or a girl friend who spoke a soothing language on her lips, and not this doleful, guttural Hebrew.

But some impression was made. It was made by the strange way in which Jesus died. Paid to watch though they were, they couldn't help watching; they saw a man in his prime offer no resistance to the cross. They heard him pray forgiveness for themselves, the very men who pinned him there. Perhaps they felt shabby crucifying *him*. Perhaps they would have liked to let him go. But this they never dared to do, it would have meant the cross for them instead, for as in the Prussian army, so in the Roman, those whom the rank and file feared most were their own officers. So they crucified him, and we need not be surprised to read thereafter that sitting down they watched him there. . . . But he didn't linger as most victims lingered. Nor did he sink slowly into unconsciousness as most victims sank. There was a strong cry at the end, "It is finished." And there was a confident committal as if the victim was taking his own leave, "Father, into thy hands I commend my spirit." That is what they saw. I say, I do not know what impression it made, but it made some. The centurion standing over against the cross said, "Truly this man was the Son of God."

68

We're all busy these days, talking about Summit conferences, talking about the General Election, talking about shorter skirts or longer skirts, talking about the latest murder. There are flats to be found, and holidays to be planned. There are worries in business. There are problems at home. Mary's got a boy friend. John has got a girl friend. There's old age to cope with, and illness to cope with, and who knows what the Budget will bring forth. I don't know what impression Good Friday makes on all this, I don't know what impression the Cross. Life goes jostling on. People are born, people marry, people die . . . perhaps many are simply like the soldiers who seeing the Cross do not know what it is they see. It makes some impression, but not much, and life goes on again. . . .

And then there were the mockers. Perhaps the centurions didn't mock, but some men did. The passers-by mocked. The chief priests, elders and scribes mocked. And at the start of the crucifixion both malefactors crucified with Jesus also mocked. They mocked at this for an idea of a Saviour, a man on a cross. They mocked at this for an idea of God, a carpenter on wood with nails he couldn't use. It was his impotence they laughed at—just as if anything strung up like a rat *could* be God, just as if God could have a body at all, just as if there is any sense whatever in speaking of God as a Person. . . .

To the mockers the Crucifixion is Christianity's own advertisement of its own stupidity. And such mockers are with us still. Believe in a God if you must, but in the name of all common sense let it be a God that is a power behind the universe; or a power immanent in nature; or the Life force, or the Evolutionary tendency, or the sum total of all existence—but an old man in the sky or a young man on a cross, what antiquated mythology! What evidence of human stupidity!

And now a third group by the Cross—mentioned by John —a group of women. Quite a company according to the records: Mary the mother of Jesus was there—she'd be middle-aged by now, she had aged in a week; with her, her sister, and Mary the wife of Clopas, and Mary Magdalene, possibly much younger. *They* saw nothing to mock at. They saw something to *cry* over. Presently they saw a man, maybe in his twenties, lead his aunt, the mother of Jesus, close to the cross, as close as the guard would allow, close enough to speak. And they did speak. But she couldn't bear it. The young man led her back to the city, doubtless to weep alone, for the young man reappeared once more. All this from a distance the women saw. That was their Good Friday— an exhibition of man's cruelty to man. And what would it give them but a sacred memory to carry locked in their hearts for ever—there once was a man years ago, of lovely life, of lovely face. Oh, thank God for all women who are tender, what would this earth be without the tenderness of women—but Christianity is not the tender memory of a lovely man who lived so long ago. There's no energy in that, no religion in that, nothing to buoy a man up when he faces his death or faces his sins.

And then there was the young man, whose name was John, the only Apostle to be there. What did he see? And there was Simon of Cyrene, who had carried the cross, what did he see? And Joseph of Arimathea who later went to beg the body from Pilate—what did he see? And Barabbas, set free from prison, if he joined the trooping crowds to troop and see the cross on which he might have hung himself—what did he see? Of all these with the soldiers it might be written: "And sitting down they watched him there." What did they see?

And as we look out from our world of Summit conferences, of elections, of shorter skirts or longer skirts, and wage demands—what do we see? Someone to mock at? No. Someone to weep over? That's all too long ago, and sorrows since have piled on sorrows. Someone who was faithful unto death? That is something, it is a great deal in our modern world. There is far too little faithfulness when it comes to making demands—people hive off too easily, to another woman, to another man, to another job, to another fiddle, to a lower ideal—stickability has gone, stickability which costs. If this afternoon[1] sitting down we watch a man who was faithful to his death, that is a needed lesson to learn in this, our modern slippery age.

What do we see? A man sufficiently great, sufficiently poised, sufficiently calm to receive the kiss of a traitor without revenge, to behold the misunderstanding of his disciples without reproof, to be uncowed in the presence of authority, to be dignified as he treads the final road. Here's a man's ideal—no whimpers, no recriminations, no obsequiousness of any kind. That's worth seeing. Would to God we saw it more.

But still we haven't seen the real significance. And this we never shall till we see it from the other side of Christ's Resurrection from the grave. Then what do we see? Not a man to mock at, but a God to marvel at: not a man to weep over, but a God to exalt over. For this is God in human form. God as he ever was, God as he ever will be. God who never leaves men, not though they mock at him, spit on him, crucify him, or weep over him. God loves beyond the last limit. He loves Judas, he loves Caiaphas, Pilate, the staring mob, the soldiers sitting by the cross. God loves us busy with our Summit conferences, by-elections, shorter skirts and endless wage demands. That is what sitting down at Calvary we should see: "God so loved the world that he gave his only begotten Son that whosoever believeth in him should not perish but have eternal life." That is why we call it Good Friday, that is why we have no tears to shed. They are swallowed up in wonder. God loves sufficiently to forbear—that is redemptive if only we will see it, redemptive if only we will take it. . . .

[1] Good Friday afternoon. The Three Hours Service, Westminster Abbey.

10. ROYAL RELIGION

St. Matthew, Chapter 28, vv. 16-20

But the eleven disciples went into Galilee, unto the mountain where Jesus had appointed them. And when they saw him, they worshipped him: but some doubted.

And Jesus came to them and spake unto them, saying, All authority hath been given unto me in heaven and on earth. Go ye therefore, and make disciples of all the nations, baptizing them into the name of the Father and of the Son and of the Holy Ghost: teaching them to observe all things whatsoever I commanded you: and lo, I am with you alway, even unto the end of the world.

<hr>

MATTHEW 28, vv. 18-20: And Jesus came to them and spake unto them, saying, All authority hath been given unto me in heaven and on earth. Go ye therefore, and make disciples of all the nations, baptizing them into the name of the Father and of the Son and of the Holy Ghost: teaching them to observe all things whatsoever I commanded you: and lo, I am with you alway, even unto the end of the world.

<hr>

I AM not quite sure that Jesus *did* say these words. No New Testament scholar is quite sure. I might not have made a remark like this four years ago when I first began to occupy this pulpit, but I think you trust me now, and you know I am no destructive critic of the sacred scriptures. I hold them in far too high a regard for that. But we must apply our minds to them. We are supposed to be adult in our Christian thinking, and we must admit that the phrase "the name of the Father, and of the Son, and of the Holy Ghost" has an ecclesiastical ring about it. It looks as if Church custom has been "read back" into the words of Jesus, and developed Church custom at that; because many years elapsed before the Church baptized into the name of this grand Trinitarian formula; in the early days baptism took place simply into the name of the Lord Jesus.

I am not worried about this "reading back", and I don't want you to be worried by it. It is for this very reason that I mention it because it is one of my duties to try, if I can, to stabilise your faith. What we have here in these last three verses of St. Matthew's gospel may not be the actual words of Jesus but a summary of the religion which his coming brought. As St. Matthew looked back over the years, perhaps fifty years of Church life, this is what he knew Christians experienced in their lives. This in fact is what the life, death, and resurrection of Jesus makes for—a royal religion. A religion in which there is enterprise, and a religion in which there is a sense of divine companionship.

Some time ago I was arrested by the sight of two vehicles standing almost side by side in a car park. They were both cars. In each case their owners expected to, and would in fact, ride home in them. But one was an old Austin 7 of about the 1935 variety, almost tied together with string; the other was an ultra-modern Rolls-Royce fit for service in the royal household.

And religions vary likewise. They vary astonishingly. For some their religion is little more than a vague sentimental awareness that there must be a God somewhere; it scarcely possesses even carrying power. And at the other extreme there are people with a royal religion, a religion which controls them, energises them and supports them.

And you ask me what the marks are of a royal religion. And the first I have to tell you is authority.

A few days ago I was addressed by someone who asked me if I was aware of the steady stream of converts to the Roman Catholic Church. I am constantly being asked this. I *am* aware of it; and I am also aware of the number of Roman Catholics joining the Church of England. But let that pass.

What interests us is the *reason* for people joining the Roman Catholic Church. It is because of its authoritarian character. It tells its members exactly what to believe and exactly what to do. And there *must* be authority in religion. But I do not think it resides in an infallible Church any more than I think it resides in an infallible Bible. The authority resides in the exalted Christ: "All authority hath been given unto me in heaven and on earth."

I want to stress this authority of Christ. A man has no real religion, a man has no royal religion, unless he knows himself to be under authority. It is a freely accepted authority. There is no compulsion about it. A man puts himself under it. But when he has done so there is an obligation upon him to ask, in all the affairs of his life, What will Christ have me to do? It applies to *all* the affairs of our daily life: to business, to pleasure, whom a man shall marry, what money shall he spend, what money shall he give away. The Church cannot tell you exactly. I *will* not tell you exactly. We can at best give guidance only in the way of principles. The task for the Church and its ministers is to put us all in touch with Christ himself so that we know within our inmost souls what we each should do. This is religion with authority— authority so strong that Jesus said that if ever there should come a time when a man has to decide between the closest member of his own family and Christ, he is to decide for Christ. "All authority hath been given unto me"—willingly to accept this, this is royal religion.

*   *   *

And now a *second* lesson from these closing verses of St. Matthew's gospel. Religion of the royal kind pursues a steady task. We need to note this. Our Lord has not merely given us something to believe; he has given us something to do.

Here in these verses it is set down in one grand sweep of world-wide enterprise—"Go ye therefore, and make disciples of all the nations, baptizing them into the name of the Father and of the Son and of the Holy Ghost: teaching them to observe all things whatsoever I commanded you."

74

We ought to notice this word "baptize". It roots Christian discipleship in the Church. Baptism is not an "optional extra". You cannot say, "I will be a Christian but I will have nothing to do with the Church." We ought also to notice the phrase "baptizing them into the name of . . ." It is a strange phrase, but in old Greek papyri it is used for money transactions; one man putting his money into the name of another. Thus he gained security. And when you and I were baptized, we were openly declared to be, what we in fact are, under the security of the care of God.

So now we see what making disciples means. It means baptizing and teaching. And not only in South Kensington, but in all the world. And wherever religion is of the royal variety it is active in this way. It has a task to perform, an enterprise to engage in. That is why the true Church is always a missionary-minded Church. That is why the true Christian is always keen to draw his neighbours to the faith which means so much to him. If we have concern only for ourselves we fail, yes, even in the end fail to help ourselves; but if we care for others' needs we find we, too, are stronger . . . and this is royal religion, religion with a mission.

* * *

Thirdly there is the fact of the divine presence. "Lo, I am with you alway, even unto the end of the world."

I wonder if you have said to someone at some time (I am sure you must have done), to someone perhaps setting off on a journey, to someone about to undergo an operation, to someone engaging in a few days on some particularly difficult piece of work: "I'll be thinking of you." You long to be there with that other person, helping, sustaining and encouraging, but you cannot be, at least not in bodily presence, so you say, "I'll be thinking of you." And it does help. It helps to know we are not forgotten. As it happens, it may help far more positively than that, for telepathy is very real. . . .

And what I have to say this morning is that religion of the royal kind is one which feels that God has not forgotten.

75

And this in the end is what we chiefly need. Not a philosophy of life, not even a theology, and certainly not an explanation of our troubles. What we need is someone to hold our hand as we journey through. "Yea, though I walk through the valley of the shadow of death, I will fear no evil for thou art with me, thy rod and thy staff comfort me." This is real religion. This is royal religion. When I am lonely —knowing in my bones that Christ has not forgotten me. When I am frustrated, when I cannot, try as I may, straighten all my problems out; when I am struggling hard to make my way in life—to feel that God is on my side, this is royal religion. And this is Christianity. It is bound up with the very name of Christ, you have it in the first chapter of St. Matthew's gospel: "Immanuel, God with us," and you have it in the last: "Lo, I am with you alway, even unto the end of the world."

"Christ within me, Christ behind me, Christ before me, Christ beside me, Christ to win me, Christ to comfort and restore me."

This is royal religion. I cannot prove it to you. I can only bear my testimony, humble as it is. A man has a real religion when he feels that God has not forgotten him.

*   *   *

And so I think of the Church here for which I am responsible. I think of my own ministry for which I am accountable. Have I commended real religion? Have I commended royal religion? We can tell, all of us, by looking for the marks: a religion in which there is authority, a religion in which there is an outreaching enterprise, and a religion in which there is a sense of the divine presence. I hope with all my heart I have commended this, for only this is "carrying" religion.

76

PART TWO

TWO SERIES OF OLD TESTAMENT STUDIES

I. The Requirements of Leadership: Three Old Testament Character Studies

1. SAUL THE GIFTED

ONE day the committee of which I am a member was puzzled. Our task was to appoint a teacher for a Church school overseas. We were puzzled because only one candidate applied, and it was desperate that the post be filled. The candidate had excellent technical qualifications, clearly he was a gifted man; yet we doubted the reality of his Christian profession. But we took a chance on it. We appointed him. But we made a mistake, a bad mistake. In spite of his gifts, the man failed miserably and left a train of problems in his wake.

I have wondered since if the failure of King Saul can be explained along these lines. I know Saul isn't easy to interpret. Nothing about Saul is easy. Not even his bare history is easy to trace. There are two accounts of his election to the kingship, an earlier and a later, as any modern commentary will demonstrate; and if they are difficult to reconcile, they are more difficult to expound. Was Saul the King of God's choice? Could such a man as this be thought to be the one that God would crown? If the later account of his election to the kingship (I Samuel 8, vv. 4-22) represents later thoughts on Saul, it would seem that there was doubt on this question. Yet Samuel chose Saul, and, having chosen him, encouraged high hopes in him (I Samuel 10, v. 1). So much so that Saul only needed to wait quietly at home till the opportunity to prove his leadership and have it accepted by the people presented itself. And this happened when Nahash the Ammonite threatened Jabesh-Gilead (I Samuel 11, vv. 1-11, 15). So Saul, according to the earlier account, became King. His natural gifts, perceived by Samuel, were part of the reason; and he came, too, of an outstanding family.

"Now there was a man of Benjamin whose name was Kish, the son of Abiel, the son of Zeror, the son of Becorath, the son of Aphiah, the son of Benjamin, a mighty man of valour. And he had a son whose name was Saul, a young man and a goodly: and there was not among the children of Israel a goodlier person than he: from his shoulders and upward he was higher than any of the people" (I Samuel 9, vv. 1, 2).

Physical excellence is impressive. If a man lacks it, some compensating factor must be prominent in his personality or he will not lead. But Saul was "goodly" with a goodliness no one in Israel surpassed. We shall see, too, that his successor was also "goodly to look upon" (I Samuel 16, v. 12). Physical excellence is important for leadership. So is youth and so is energy. They are pure gifts in life, and Saul possessed them. Whether nature's gifts for leadership are sufficient to support leadership is the chief question we need to ask. It is the question the story of Saul should *make* us ask. Whether Samuel asked it we do not know. It is doubtful if the people did. Another matter was clamouring for attention—Nahash the Ammonite threatening Jabesh-Gilead. And Saul, doubtless with Samuel's words burning in his mind (I Samuel 10, v. 1) arose to lead a strong resistance. Every man's cattle should be destroyed if he did not join the resistance (I Samuel 11, v. 7). This is leadership: strong, natural, worldly leadership. And the Hebrews recognised it. They rallied. They repelled Nahash. And they returned to clamour for Saul as King (I Samuel 11, v. 15). He was by then not only Samuel's choice but the people's choice, though none but those ever ready to confuse *vox populi* with *vox dei* would dare to assert that this of necessity also made him God's choice.

Now if you are a popular leader you must succeed. And Saul did. He succeeded in conflict with the Philistines. To do so was the need of the hour, for this Aegean people, settling on Canaan's maritime plain (and thus giving their name to Palestine) had driven across the plain of Aesdraelon, splitting the land of Hebrew conquest into two. Nothing more was needed then than unified action to drive these people out. But hitherto the Hebrews had lacked the will for unity. To his cost Gideon had already found this out. His attempt to found a kingship had ended in disaster (Judges 9). Then the time was not ripe as now it seemed to be ripe. Saul saw it and seized it, and his act confirmed him in his kingship.

We ought not to underrate the benefits of natural leadership. We ought not to underrate the achievements of Saul. Without Saul there would have been no David. Without David there would have been no ideal of kingship to inspire nations of a Messianic King. Look at Saul's achievements! Ephraim and Benjamin united. Some authority gained over Judah and even the territory east of Jordan. And, since he was slain on Mount Gilboa, it is reasonable to assume that he was campaigning in the north in order to attempt reunion with the tribes cut off by the Philistine break-through in the northern plain.

And not only did the people admire Saul, they loved him. This is clear from the fact that after he was slain the men of Jabesh-Gilead took their lives in their hands to save his shattered body from the turrets of Beth-Shan and give it decent burial (I Samuel 31, v. 8f.). You don't do that unless you love. You don't do that when a man is all but mad before he comes to die unless you greatly loved. But the people never forgot the Saul they chose when Nahash threatened Jabesh-Gilead, and they loved him till the end.

And yet Saul failed. That is the puzzle. It is also the tragedy. Your heart could almost break to hear him ask, if not in words, yet with this implication: "What more could I have done in Israel than I have done in it?"

Why did Saul fail? Is it because he lacked in heart the heart of religion? We can but wonder when we read that as a youth he did not even know the whereabouts of Samuel (I Samuel 9). It is true that Samuel may not have been a prophet of the national standing the later accounts purport to make him; but for the son of a powerful sheik not to know the local seer makes us wonder how much, how little, religion possessed Saul's heart. I put it kindly, but I do put it, that when, for example, a young man wishes to get married but does not so much as know the name of the local minister of religion, you cannot blame me if I wonder how much religion, if any, resides in his heart. Externals do count.

Furthermore, when Saul did display religious fervour in imitation of the prophets, the surprise of the people—"Is Saul also among the prophets?" (I Samuel 10, v. 11)—does not encourage belief in the spiritual awareness of this man. Apparently a religious experience was the last experience he was expected to portray.

But was he perchance converted? Is this the meaning of I Samuel 10, v. 9: "God gave him another heart." I do not know; but if ever he came close to conversion, it was at the moment of his anointing (I Samuel 10, v. 1). Many people on the threshold of some forward step in life, such as a couple before their wedding-day, are sensitive to God as not before. But with many, and I would hazard a guess with Saul, the occasion passes and the sensitivity passes. And in the case of Saul, in place of an inner awareness of God, there came to be mere conformity in religion. . . . If this is so, his end is not surprising.

But is it so? We look at the man. *First*, to the occasion when Samuel failed to arrive and offer the sacrifice before the battle with the Philistines (I Samuel 13, v. 8f.); so Saul offered it and was rejected in his Kingdom (v. 14). I do not think the significance of this incident is either retribution for law-breaking or judgment upon presumption. I think it is a window on Saul's hypocrisy of heart—"I forced myself therefore and offered the burnt offering" (v. 12). We ought of course to pause before we ever call a man a hypocrite, but Saul bears many marks. Can we think that in his mind the battle would turn upon that sacrifice? Was a sacrifice needed when Nahash was attacking? But then he wasn't King as now he is King. So the rites must be observed. Religion binds tribes into a nation, especially Hebrew tribes; you cannot neglect it. So we see into Saul's heart. Religion is a means, a thing to use for temporal advantage. Saul is no convert in religion. He is a conformist to religion. Saul is the gifted worldly leader who thinks to rope religion in his schemes, but of its essence he knows very little.

Secondly, we see in the King a perverted sense of justice. We see it in a story of rashness and self-assertion (I Samuel 14). Saul made a rash vow before a battle with the Philistines: "Cursed be any man that eateth any food until it be evening, and I be avenged on mine enemies" (v. 24). That is rash. It is also senseless. There are vows enough in life that ought to be made without adding to their number. (Puritans please note.) And to prohibit fighting men from eating food while the battle is on (providing the battle is not hindered) is only worth the label "crass stupidity". And Jonathan, Saul's son, transgressed. Jonathan who that day had served with great distinction. It was unwitting transgression. He had not heard when the command was given. Yet Saul demanded that he be slain. And yet he was not slain. The *people* rescued him, rescued him from his father! Saul's religion was of the kind there was need to rescue from! Such was its condemnation by the people—"Shall Jonathan die, who hath wrought this great salvation in Israel? God forbid: as the Lord liveth there shall not one hair of his head fall to the ground; for he hath wrought this day with God" (v. 45).

Not that the matter ended there. Starved as the soldiers were when at last they won the day, "they flew upon the spoil and took sheep and oxen and calves and slew them on the ground: and the people did eat them with the blood" (v. 32). We do not know what external law they broke in doing this, but they broke into their consciences. Yet Saul had no perception of himself as causing this. Charging *them* with treachery (and not himself for foolishness), he presumed to make provision for their right behaviour. A great stone was to be set where the beasts must be killed and the blood be drained away. Such was Saul's religion, attention to forms, but blind to context, a thing useful in the art of government. And so on this occasion he "built an altar unto the Lord"

83

the first he ever built (v. 35). Occasions are not wanting when irreligious leaders have thought it wise to help support the Church. But it isn't religion that is in the forefront of their minds. It never was with Saul.

Thirdly, we come to an incident, which, unlike the other two, belongs to the late strand of historical material. But this too sets its finger on the same defect in this man's character. It is the notorious incident embarrassing to most, Samuel's command to Saul—"Go and smite Amalek, and utterly destroy all that they have and spare not" (I Samuel 15, v. 3). And yet how shall we who have engaged in obliteration bombing and manufactured nuclear weapons dogmatise? Surely only those who are clear in mind on what *we* ought to do . . . But let us turn to Saul. Was his disobedience of Samuel's command a case of secular enlightenment rebelling against the senseless taboos of religion? Could it be Saul's innate kindness reacting against Samuel's religious fanaticism? And we must be frank. Samuel's action is shocking. "Then said Samuel, Bring ye hither to me Agag the king of the Amalekites. And Agag came unto him delicately. And Agag said, Surely the bitterness of death is past. And Samuel said, As the sword hath made women childless, so shall thy mother be childless among women. And Samuel hewed Agag in pieces before the Lord in Gilgal" (I Samuel 15, vv. 32, 33).

The action of Samuel, a priest, is shocking in itself. It is more shocking still in the light of some words of St. Paul. "Avenge not yourselves, beloved, but give place unto the wrath of God: for it is written, Vengeance belongeth unto me: I will recompense, saith the Lord. But if thine enemy hunger feed him; if he thirst give him to drink: for in so doing thou shalt heap coals of fire upon his head" (Romans 12, vv. 19, 20). But Samuel knew nothing of this. It is doubtful if Saul knew anything either. In any case the motive for his disobedience could scarcely have been kindness for a defenceless people, since, with the exception of Agag the king, he put them all to the sword. Only the booty he preserved. All of which points to the conclusion that Saul *was* critical of

Samuel's command. He was not wrong to be critical. All the wisdom has never resided with the Church, nor all the folly with the State. But Saul should have refused to obey Samuel; instead of which he deceived Samuel, showing thus his weakness. He said, "Blessed be thou of the Lord: I have performed the commandment of the Lord" (v. 13). And what was worse, when challenged by Samuel—"What meaneth then this bleating of the sheep in mine ears?"—Saul shifted the responsibility for the preservation of the booty on to the people; and what was worse still alleged that they did it for religious purposes (supposing to appease Samuel), and in so doing used an expression which disassociated himself from Samuel's religious allegiance—"And Saul said, They have brought them from the Amalekites: for the people spared to take the best of the sheep and of the oxen to sacrifice unto the Lord *thy* God: and the rest we have utterly destroyed" (v. 15). From which we can see again how far Saul's heart was from the heart of religion. For him it was an activity to which, among a religious people, it was wise to pay attention.

Then Saul broke. His strength broke. He confessed both sin and weakness. "I have sinned: for I have transgressed the commandments of the Lord, and thy words: because I feared the people and obeyed their voice" (I Samuel 15, v. 24). But there was *no forgiveness* for Saul. We should notice this. There was no forgiveness though he asked explicitly—"Now therefore I pray thee pardon my sin, and turn thee again with me that I may worship the Lord" (v. 25). There was no forgiveness because it was not of his standing with God that he was thinking but of his standing before the people. This comes out in verse 30—"Then he said, I have sinned: yet honour me now, I pray thee, before the elders of my people and before Israel." But you cannot obtain God's forgiveness if in your heart of hearts you are not concerned with him. This Samuel knew, and hence his hard reply—"I will not return with thee: for thou hast rejected the word of the Lord, and the Lord hath rejected thee from being King over Israel" (v. 26).

85

All this makes solemn reading. It shows the peril of trifling with religion. It shows how a man may arrive at a position at which religion has nothing to say. Such was the experience of Herod Antipas in the gospel records. From being a man who heard John the Baptist "gladly" (St. Mark 6, v. 20), he became one to whom Jesus had nothing to say (St. Luke 23, vv. 8, 9). Sin may in fact be unpardonable. Not because God is unwilling. Nor because any sin is too heinous. That is not true. But because when a man has, for his own nefarious ends, deliberately confused moral distinctions, he may arrive in the end (if he persists) at a place where moral distinctions are unrecognisable. At that place forgiveness no longer makes sense. It cannot be received. Sin can become *psychologically* unpardonable. The case is like an air-pilot unable to receive messages from his base since he has destroyed his own instrument panel.

So Saul became a reject. Lacking in his heart the heart of religion, he sought to manipulate its externals to bolster up the kingship, till in the end he knew no other way. Thus we see him on the day of his rejection, pleading with Samuel for honour in public. Before the people at least he must worship the Lord: before the people at least Church and State must walk together, even if the Lord is Samuel's God and not his own (I Samuel 15, v. 30). And Samuel agreed. For the people's sake the sham must be perpetuated. Saul worshipped, but not in his heart. Saul and Samuel were seen together, but in spirit they were worlds apart. Yet Saul continued. Call this courage if you will, but it is courage born of desperation. He had lost his bearings, and for all his plunging on, his life could only end in dismal tragedy.

But the end was not yet. Moral deterioration is a process. It takes time. But the outcome in "goodly men" is as mean as that in any lesser sort. Saul became morose (I Samuel 16, v. 4). And his servants, who doubtless bore the brunt of this as servants do, sought to soothe his soul with instruments of music. It was an external remedy for an internal disease. No wonder it failed. But the upshot was (according to one account) that David found himself brought to Saul to play

86

upon his harp (I Samuel 16, v. 23). And Saul grew to love David. And love can redeem. It can redeem better than music. But Saul was not redeemed. His love turned sour. It turned to jealousy. It took that turn when the crowds acclaimed David as the conqueror of the Philistines' champion.

> Saul hath slain his thousands,
> And David his ten thousands.   (I Samuel 18, v. 7.)

And then his jealousy developed a murderous intent. He hunted David; and in this hunt alienated his son and alienated his daughter, and smeared his hands with the blood of eighty-five priests: nor did he spare, this time, women and children, sucklings and oxen, he slew them all in the city of priests (I Samuel 22, vv. 18, 19).

Then to this man, with his darkened mind, the end came; but not before he had had recourse to degenerate religion (I Samuel 28, v. 3f.), the only kind to comfort an irreligious man. We call it spiritualism. But the results were barren. He only heard of his own extinction on the following day of battle. Even so he went. The kingdom must continue. The Philistines must be attacked. For this he was crowned. For this he must die. A gifted king, a courageous king, a rejected king, a king who knew no real religion . . . but a king who did his duty; yet that is not sufficient.

* * *

Was he the king whom God had chosen? How can we doubt it! But not for Saul's gifts alone was this choice made, but because he also had it in him to rise to spiritual stature. But he did not take his opportunity. It came, as it often comes, on the threshold of a new life. It came at his anointing. At that moment he was sensitive to God, so sensitive as to appear also "among the prophets" (I Samuel 10, v. 11). His call was a double one; the kingship over men and the service of God. To respond to both was his only hope of success; but he responded only to the former. Thus he lost both throne and soul, a reject who, because he *would* not listen to the

87

voice of God, found himself at last incapable of listening to the voice of God. So he quits the page of history, warning as he goes how serious is the call of God to any man. Hear it and we are never the same again. Either we rise or we fall. We do not stay at the place we occupy.

And one last thought. No man, be he as gifted as Saul, as courageous as Saul, as popular as Saul, no man with impunity can use religion for his schemes. Saul may be King, but God is final King. Religion touches realities, not shams. "He that falleth on this stone shall be broken to pieces: but on whomsoever it shall fall it will scatter him as dust" (Matthew 21, v. 44). So said Jesus of the invisible kingdom of God. It is a hard saying. But it serves to remind us that in dealing with religion we are dealing with absolutes that cannot be for ever tampered with. We must be honest when we deal with God, but if we are—and this is the light which shines on the farther side of the tragedy of Saul—in the love of God not even our sins will spell our final overthrow.

2. DAVID THE SPIRITUALLY-MINDED

I HOPE you do not count it waste of time to think of kings who lived so long ago—Saul, David, Solomon. I am a busy man, and you are busy people, and I would share your doubts were I not certain that these kings are people you may meet, even in the Gloucester Road, or peering at yourself one morning through the looking-glass.

David isn't easy to see; that is my apology now for using up your time. And I do not think we shall even start to see him straight unless we've plumbed the depths of Saul. I mean, I do not reckon we shall know what David had unless we understand what Saul had *not*. We might even prefer Saul. After all, as far as we know, he never fell a victim to any kind of Bathsheba, nor was there rebellion in his house. Yet Saul was rejected, and David was accepted. . . .

We shall have to notice David's origin. In a sense it was humble, and the early conditions of his life were hard. But we must neither over-emphasise nor dramatise the importance of these facts. A pinched beginning may mean a pinched ending in spite of later wealth acquired. Hardships in youth and silver spoons at birth do not inevitably make for subsequent greatness. They are conditioned by another factor which we must make it our purpose to uncover.

David of course had gifts. No man rises to be a leader of his fellows if lacking in all gifts. Of David, it is recorded that he was "goodly to look upon", special mention being made of his hair and his eyes (I Samuel 16, v. 12). This made him attractive to women when coupled with his manliness, not least to the Princess Michal, daughter of king Saul, who fell in love at sight with what she saw before her eyes. But she never understood his inner feelings. She never knew his heart. Like father, like daughter; she was defective in all spiritual awareness. So her love could never last, nor did it

89

last, it turned to utter loathing (II Samuel 6, v. 16). Love rarely lasts where spiritual affinity plays no binding part. All this is seen in contrast in the friendship of Jonathan and David. They loved each other till death because their "souls were knit" (I Samuel 18, v. 1).

David was attractive to men as well as women. And not only this, but he had a feeling for the use of words revealing a poetic nature. Of course we do not know how many Psalms he wrote within our Psalter, but it is unlikely he has written none. There is his lament over Saul (II Samuel 1, v. 19ff.) to testify to his gift, and his lament over Abner (II Samuel 3, vv. 33, 34). There is nothing to cast doubt on the Davidic authorship of these poems; indeed, the very fact that they contain no reference to Yahweh, nor any reference to the special place which David held among the Hebrew people, makes it unlikely that they have been invented and attributed to David. We may then accept the tradition that he was "the sweet Psalmist of Israel" (II Samuel 23, v. 1), and since Psalms were in essence musical compositions, in their simplest form sung as they were composed, we may count David not only of a poetic nature but musical as well.

These gifts combine, but the martial qualities which he also possessed added up, if not to an unknown, certainly to a rare, assembly of skills. In our day we have met poets who were soldiers and scholars able to conduct guerilla warfare. Of all such David, with his outward beauty, poetic gifts and musical gifts, coupled with capacity as captain of a band of outlaws, was undoubtedly the father.

This was David's natural greatness that he held within himself seemingly contrasted attributes. The book of Samuel sets them out in no uncertain terms. He was "cunning in playing (the harp), and a mighty man of valour, and a man of war, and prudent in speech and a comely person" (I Samuel 16, v. 18). He was in this the Renaissance ideal. And such makes for leadership. It makes for an appeal to diverse groups of people. No one-track mind, no genius even, can ever be a leader of the people, nor any single-gifted man. All of which is why a leader may be surpassed by this or that subordinate in this or that qualification, and still be qualified to lead. If you are looking for a leader you must look at your candidate as a whole and at his *combination* of abilities.

But beware of men (and women) with gifts alone if this is all they have. Far from leading a people, they may trouble a people. Not that gifted men are not required. Nor can it be thought that piety "will do". Pity the Church with leaders who are good but also lacking in all gifts. But men possessing nothing else but gifts are men to be avoided. Of such a group David certainly did not partake.

* * *

And so we turn to think what David had which Saul, the gifted, did not have. We turn to think of this to find the key to David's special greatness.

First turn to an early interview between these men. Saul was refusing David's request to go and fight Goliath: "Thou art not able to go against this Philistine to fight with him, for thou art but a youth, and he a man of war from his youth" (I Samuel 17, v. 33). And this is what the youthful David said: "The Lord that delivered me out of the paw of the lion, and out of the paw of the bear, he will deliver me out of the hand of this Philistine" (v. 37). Evidently David was drawing on experience—"Thy servant kept his father's sheep, and when there came a lion or a bear and took a lamb out of the flock, I went out after him and smote him and delivered him out of his mouth: and when he arose against me, I caught him by his beard and smote him and slew him. Thy servant slew both the lion and the bear" (vv. 34-36).

Youthful religious experience is often crudely told, there is an element of bombast and an air of intolerance. But if it is genuine, and if in later life it broadens out, mellowing with age, it may be the key to a great man's greatness, it may be the keystone, upholding his gifts.

Next we see David rising to power. He did not attain it by goodness alone. There was astuteness and there was caution; there was patience, and there was energy. If, as must have seemed probable, the throne would one day come to him, he did nothing which might hinder it. After all he had married the King's daughter, and the only rival to the throne was Ishbosheth, and he incompetent. So when a slave appeared with King Saul's bracelet, taken from the dead King's hand (II Samuel 1, v. 10), David shewed himself defender of the dead King's memory, he slew the slave at once. This showed how much he valued popular esteem. Nor was it only from a heart of sorrow that he uttered his lament over Saul and Jonathan slain upon the field of battle, he also had an eye to general reactions.

There was also caution. If David knew the maxim "Make hay while the sun shines", he also knew the wisdom embodied in the proverb "Everything comes to him who knows how to wait for it". So he waited. First he set his throne in Hebron in the south (II Samuel 2, v. 4). All was very modest. Ishbosheth in Mahanaim reigned with Abner's strength. In fact, so modest was his kingdom that even the Philistines were unalerted, and certainly his rival Ishbosheth showed no concern. Why should they when David lacked a mighty stronghold and Jebus stood there safe in hostile hands?

But David was waiting, waiting on events. This waiting we should also notice as well as youthful piety. David did not force the pace; and for all his scheming, all his caution, he took good care his hands were clean. And so we see him sparing Saul when he could have struck him to the ground (I Samuel 24, v. 4., and 26, v. 8); nor did he have his rival murdered. But the day came when both were dead, both come to a violent end. For this David had waited, and when it happened, he was ready, ready for the kingship.

He was ready, too, for action. Action was necessary. The Philistines, alerted by the death of David's rival, feared the power which David now would wield. And so they struck with all their force in the centre, overrunning David's strongholds. Even so, they failed to bring him to their heels. He fled to the mountains in which he'd learned the tactics of guerilla warfare. And then he took the fortress of Jerusalem, after which his adversaries had lost their opportunities.

We need to notice Jerusalem. Not simply because its

92

capture was a military feat. Not simply because it gave the King a stronghold none could hope to overthrow, and one with independence of all tribal jealousy. But Jerusalem had religious significance. It had an ancient history of the worship of El Elyon, God Most High, and a priest-king named Melchizedek. So we sense the thoughts that grew in David's mind, thoughts of the kingship, lofty thoughts, unique thoughts, utterly unique thoughts in any oriental land, and perhaps unique in shaping kingship in the West. The kingship in Israel was to be a sacred office, God, king and the people united in one sacred tie, each with obligations; and later still thoughts of "sacramental kingship", later taken up in Autumn Festivals, the Feasts of Tabernacles. So Jerusalem, David's city, entered Hebrew history, a witness to Yahweh, a witness for ever.

> Walk about Zion and go round about her: and tell the towers
> thereof.
> Mark well her bulwarks, set up her houses
> That ye may tell them that come after.
> For this God is our God for ever and ever:
> He will be our guide even unto death.

> (Psalm 48, vv. 11-13.)

And not only did David's city enter Hebrew history, but Christian theology, and even eschatology. It became the symbol of the goal of life, the heavenly Jerusalem, the new Jerusalem, "Jerusalem the golden, with milk and honey blest."

And then his hope to build a house of cedar wood fit for God to dwell in (II Samuel 7, v. 2). This in itself was an indication of the character of David. We need to think how little hope of such a project ever lay within the mind of Saul. But a more important fact to note is the spirit of this man on being told that he would never build this temple, but his son to follow him (v. 13). To accept the will of God without resentment is a greater sign of greatness than to wish to build a noble temple. And David had come to terms with it. He had come to terms with the principle of acceptance. He knew that what we cannot change in life must never be resented. Nor is the highest way the way of resignation. Acceptance is the answer, acceptance in faith, in faith that down beneath the deep frustration there lies some purpose in the mind of God adopted for our good. And the blunt rebuke for sin against Uriah (II Samuel 12, v. 7ff.). David accepted it. And the bereavement of the child of Bathsheba. This in faith he too accepted (v. 23). And for his "numbering the people" (II Samuel 24, v. 10), considered then a sharp transgression, David bowed his head—"Let us fall into the hands of God for his mercies are great." This is the principle of acceptance. It characterises David, nor shall we ever plumb his greatness unless we note it well.

Wherein lay the secret of king David's greatness? Not in his gifts, unusual as they were. Not in his achievements, spectacular as they must have been, judging from the sparse accounts which intrigue us to know more; nor even was king David famous for a life of moral purity. But he had what Saul lacked—spiritual awareness. There was in him a feeling after God, a feeling after the hand of God in human destiny. This is spiritual-mindedness. He had it in youth, he had it as king, an inner conviction that God had called him to the throne (II Samuel 7, vv. 8, 18). And when a man is aware of this he accepts in faith the turns of fortune life serves up to him. This is spiritual-mindedness. This is the key to David. This is why the scripture calls him "a man after God's own heart" (I Samuel 13, v. 14; Acts 13, v. 22). For all his faults and all his failures, David wished to do God's will. It is what we wish that indicates our heart. It is what we want that justifies us in the sight of God. Because of this, this king was justified, or counted righteous, in the sight of God, not for works of mercy he had done.

* * *

And yet for all his heart and all his head and all the lofty heights to which he drew this little people, making them the most renowned in all the land of Syria, David fell from eminence. He fell through crude instincts in his human

94

nature. Not that he ought not to have had them. Not that instincts in themselves have any moral taint. Instincts are the raw material of our earthbound life, the means by which the race survives; but raw they always are, and discipline they always need. So never count the man of God as lacking in male instincts. The man of God is never half a man, but a raw man refined by discipline in constant touch with God. The truth is, love of God and vital instincts co-exist within the self-same man albeit bringing tension. And so long as man is master of himself, his instincts are a driving force, there will be no catastrophe. But when the discipline is gone, his instincts drive him on to fatal consequences, and spiritual-mindedness will not preserve him.

This is to imply that spirituality is no substitute for morality, but only grows within its soil. To this objections have been raised, not least upon the grounds of loftier wisdom. In St. Paul's day, men wearied of the moral law in seeking after God, and earned his sharp rebuke. And in our day there has been sneering at the drabness of the moral life as if it spelt restriction of a higher culture. And so we've had our rebels, rebels for free love; but as this is now commonplace it cannot be a protest and so this rôle has passed to homo-sexuality.

But while it is true spirituality is no substitute for morality, neither are they precisely the same. A moral man may have no sense of spiritual-mindedness. Of course, identification tends to be the view of conventional religion, indeed of conventional observers of religion. But this is sheer mis-understanding. Saul was not David, nor was David Saul; and if one stands for moralism and conventional religion, the other stands for spiritual-mindedness.

Once more we look at David. Crude instincts unrefined protruded in his life. Cruelty to prisoners, a readiness to lie (a common fault with Greeks and Orientals), sensuality and notions of blood-guilt. For most men the restraints of con-vention serve to keep these faults in check. In the struggle for existence it does not pay to run amok. These curbs David knew till he obtained the kingship; but when success lay in his hands the necessity was wanting. So he lost his self-control and his spirituality was powerless to help him.

All this is told in chapters of surpassing beauty (II Samuel 11-24). A man caught by a woman who may have laid her trap for him (for Bathsheba was very masterful). A man with a conscience sensitive to other's sin but gross within himself. A man in whom affection for his children drifted on to crude infatuation. And now unable to control himself, he cannot check his household nor, finally, his kingdom. There is rebellion and adultery at home: Amnom seduces Tamar and loathes her when he's done it (II Samuel 13, v. 15). And such is life. Absalom is thirsty for revenge, but thirstier still to gain his father's kingdom. So there follows usurpation, battle, and defeat. Absalom is caught by his hair in a tree and finished with Joab's darts. Lust, blood, and violent death. All these are splashed across these pages. And that David's kingdom stood intact through all these shocks bore witness to the soundness of its constitution. But the end bore no attraction. A court filled with intrigue and an old king cherished by a Shunamite girl brought in to do her work (I Kings 1, vv. 3, 4). What drabness is here! And this is David, David the great, by spiritual-mindedness binding up his gifts. But decrepitude will come, spiritual decrepitude, moral decrepitude, unless we keep the laws of Biblical morality.

Thus David passes off the scripture page, a lesson on true greatness. It is spirituality which makes for kings and queens in every walk of life; but royalty rests in the end on plain morality, and no crown is ever safe in defiance of this fact.

3. SOLOMON THE POMPOUS

IF a little man becomes a leader, and sometimes little men do become leaders, they bamboozle you. They bamboozle you so that they may appear giant size. They dress themselves up in impressive clothes, with liberal usage of stiffening and padding; their hats are tall and their boots are big. Get hold of them if you dare, and if you can, and you only lay hold on clothes. They are like birds which are all feathers, fine feathers which make fine birds, but there isn't much flesh and bone underneath. Of this they are aware. Therefore they keep you at arm's length. In fact, you never really know them. They move at a distance, and surround themselves with all manner of barriers. And if perchance you do get through the secretaries and fix an appointment, you are disappointed at the result of the interview. Always suspect the leader who is inaccessible, he hasn't much to give you. Underneath his "build-up" he's a very little man.

This is a picture of Solomon. Remember how Jesus demolished his grandeur in one revealing sentence. Holding a wild flower in his hand, he said, "Solomon in all his glory was not arrayed like one of these." But he's built up, of course, even in the Bible. He's meant to be built up. And that's all there is to much of it—"build-up". You can't get through the drapery to the real man. Those acquainted with Old Testament criticism will know what I mean when I say the Deuteronomic writer has built him up.

But who was this Solomon? He was the son of David and Bathsheba; not conceived out of wedlock, but in wedlock, for David married Bathsheba after the death of their illegitimate child and Uriah's death. The name Solomon means "peaceful", and his alternative name, Jedidah, means "Beloved of Yah". The text, II Samuel 12, v. 24, roundly says, "And the Lord loved him." This at least cannot be denied. The Lord loves all his children, even those born of unions like David and Bathsheba's. But perhaps the phrase meant more. Perhaps it means "Where sin did abound, grace did much more abound" (Romans 5, v. 20).

We cannot overlook the disadvantages in which Solomon was born. To be born into luxury does not make for character unless precautions are taken. With Solomon they were not taken, for he knew neither hardness, nor bore the yoke in his youth. On the contrary, born late in David's life he experienced only the declining years of his father's leadership. And a home in which polygamy obtained must have been a home in which jealousy, intrigue and disrespect for women's personality also obtained. And if women are disrespected in a community, the weak are never safe. They weren't with Solomon.

We ought to examine in I Kings, chapters 1 and 2, the beginning of Solomon's reign. He was made king in a hurry. Adonijah, David's eldest son, expected to be king, but before his father's death, noting the state of the court, he counted it advisable to attempt to secure his kingship. Reckoning that his father's life was drawing to a close, this good-looking man, next in line after Absalom, received the backing of Joab and Abiathar, representing the Army and the Church. It was a formidable confederation. There was however an opposing confederation. There was Benaiah, the commander of David's bodyguard, Zadok the priest, and Nathan the prophet. The former were for Adonijah, the latter for Solomon. And the latter group worked on the dying King David, through Bathsheba, to get him installed as king at the very time when the supporters of Adonijah were feasting themselves preparatory to seizing the reins of power (I Kings 1, vv. 41-43).

In the midst of all this passion and intrigue, it is difficult to see what qualification Solomon had for leadership. It always is difficult to see Solomon! The blunt fact is that he reigned as king because David's royal bodyguard wished it to be so. The root of power in the state lay in a powerful military clique which was itself bitterly jealous of another powerful, but less powerful, clique. Solomon's accession was therefore a triumph for the principle of autocracy. He was erected on his plinth by those who saw in him the means to preserve "the status quo". All was set therefore for the office of king to be magnified.

We must note, however, that Solomon began his reign mildly. Adonijah was granted mercy. Abiathar also was allowed to live, albeit in banishment. But Joab, David's dangerous "captain of the host", was put to death, although he clung to the horns of the altar for refuge (I Kings 2, v. 28ff.). Solomon excused this by saying Joab's death had been David's wish. Adonijah did not however long enjoy the mercy granted to him. He pressed Bathsheba, who seems to have been the woman of influence at the court (she had done well for herself), to ask Solomon for David's concubine, Abishag, as his wife. These were matters Bathsheba understood. But Solomon refused. To ask for David's concubine was tantamount to making a bid for the throne. It cost Adonijah his life. Solomon forthwith sent Benaiah to execute him (I Kings 2, v. 13). One more enemy remained—the sharp-tongued Shimei. He had been ordered to build a house in Jerusalem and never to leave. But after the passage of years he broke the law to recapture two slaves, and paid the price at once by the forfeiture of his life. This action Solomon defended by calling it a return of the wickedness on his own head of that which he had shown to David (I Kings 2, v. 36ff.).

So, states the writer of the First Book of Kings, "the kingdom was established in the hand of Solomon". On which we comment—if Saul was a king after the people's heart, and David a king after God's heart, Solomon was a King after his own heart. He would do exactly as he pleased; he would become a tyrant.

* * *

Now Solomon wanted power. It must be admitted that Solomon needed power. To retain a throne that has been seized in the face of rivals who possess a claim to the throne calls for the possession of power. It must be admitted, too, that Solomon began his reign with power coupled with a commendable clemency. Adonijah was not summarily killed, nor was Shimei. There was firmness, but there was mercy. Apparently the power Solomon intended was not the power of the tyrant's sword. What he intended was to dazzle the people with magnificence.

Knowledge is power. Solomon must therefore obtain a reputation for wisdom. It would establish him in his kingdom. No one respects learning so much as those who lack it. The people must therefore come to count their King as one of superior wisdom. For wisdom Solomon prayed at Gibeon (I Kings 3, v. 9). We need to note this prayer. Nothing so reveals a man as what he prays for, and in this prayer Solomon did not pray "Lord what will thou have me to do" but "Lord what will thou give me that I may govern this people". This is equivalent to seeking God's help for what is intended already. It is praying which leaves man at the centre and God on the circumference. It is not true prayer. It is not communion with God, though this is not to say God never answers such prayers. Sometimes he does and withal sends leanness into the soul. It is a window on Solomon.

Solomon gained his reputation for wisdom, and a sample is given in I Kings 3, v. 16. We are not impressed. He proved who was the rightful mother of a child by suggesting to the two claimants that the child be cut in two and divided between them both; whereupon the true mother preferred to give the child to her rival rather than see the child killed. This action of Solomon is an example of quick-wittedness rather than wisdom. But the story would have a popular appeal. It was also useful, not only to contribute to the "build-up" of Solomon, but to suggest that he was accessible even to disputing prostitutes arguing about their illegitimate offspring. It was worth doing—once anyway.

A near modern parallel to this cleverness (as opposed to wisdom) of Solomon belongs to the late Kaiser Wilhelm of Germany. Knowing that he would meet at a banquet leading statesmen of Britain, he would labour beforehand at learning from an encyclopædia lists of facts concerning Britain—the size and tonnage of ships of the British fleet, the constitution of the London County Council, and so forth. At dinner he would select some leading but all-unsuspecting statesman and "fire off" his string of innocent questions—What was the size and tonnage of certain ships of the British fleet? What was the constitution of the London County Council? And so forth. As likely as not the unprepared statesman would flounder, whereupon the Kaiser would suggest the correct information he had already learnt, thereby giving an impression of great wisdom possessed by his Imperial Majesty the Kaiser of Germany. It used to succeed.

Kaiser Wilhelm II was a little man, and so was Solomon, but they both possessed huge reputations. Strangely enough they were both flamboyant and religiously inclined—but only in passing do we note it. Our concern is with Solomon, and his reputation is described in I Kings 4, v. 30 as follows: "And Solomon's wisdom excelled the wisdom of all the children of the East, and all the wisdom of Egypt. For he was wiser than all men; than Ethan the Ezrahite, and Heman, and Calcol, and Darda, the sons of Mahol: and his fame was in all the nations round about. And he spake three thousand proverbs: and his songs were a thousand and five. And he spake of trees, from the cedar that is in Lebanon even unto the hyssop that springeth out of the wall: he spake also of beasts and of fowl, and of creeping things and of fishes. And there came of all peoples to hear the wisdom of Solomon, from all kings of the earth, which had heard of his wisdom."

We shall be pardoned, I think, if we remark that one thousand and five songs is a large number for one man to compose, and three thousand proverbs is exceedingly large. Perhaps we are to read this as we read of Solomon building the Temple; he did not build it with his own hands, he ordered the building. Perhaps he also ordered groups of musicians and groups of "wise men" gathered in his court to compose these songs and proverbs. They were royal command works —at least they were Solomon's in this sense.

Here it must be said that God-like leadership never seeks to dazzle the led. It was the temptation Jesus refused on the pinnacle of the temple (Matthew 4, v. 5). He would not cast himself down and walk away unhurt. Such action would leave the beholders little choice but to follow him, but such following is scarcely free. It would be the outcome of an assault on the normal rational process. The truth is, the truly great leader does not need to compel people to follow him, and those who resort to all forms of "build-up" and compulsion only advertise the underlying littleness of their own stature. Such was Solomon.

* * *

A second device adopted by Solomon to dominate was his magnificent building programme. Leadership which produces buildings has something to show for itself. Buildings can in fact be the chief preoccupation of leadership of the showy kind. Clergy and schoolmasters can be trapped into this as well as governments. No one can be blamed for wondering how much of the schools policy of post-war political parties has been concerned with education; it would seem that more attention has been given to buildings. Buildings advertise. And in Church life the spiritual advance of a congregation is not so obvious, nor so permanent a memorial to a Vicar's leadership as a new Church Hall. Even a new wing for a hospital constitutes more tangible evidence of progress than does the happy healing atmosphere of the wards. New buildings need not be thus interpreted, but there is a leadership which is not strong in itself yet seeks to pass as strong and uses a showy building programme to accomplish it. Such was Solomon's.

This is not to underrate the impressiveness of his building achievement. His work meant the transformation of the very landscape at Jerusalem. Mount Moriah, north of the hill of Zion, the old Jebus, where David had dwelt, was unsuitable for building. The hill needed levelling and huge retaining walls constructed in order to effect a plain sufficiently flat to serve as a foundation. Then the intervening space between Mount Moriah and Jebus had to be filled in. When this was completed three buildings were erected; first, the house of the forest of Lebanon, next, the king's own house, and finally, the Temple surrounded by its court. All these buildings were constructed of hewn stone and cedar wood. According to modern standards, they were not large, the greatest of them being only 150 feet long, 75 feet broad and 45 feet high; but the expensive materials used and the costly furnishings, including much gold overlay, represented enormous expense. And all this must be set against a background of village life, which was all that Israel had seen of civilised life hitherto within its borders; and it must be remembered that only in David's reign did the Hebrew tribes ever experience full unity as a nation.

* * *

Truly it was a brilliant stage which Solomon had erected in the centre of his kingdom, and no doubt the people were dazzled. It is exhilarating to belong to a "go-ahead" kingdom just as it is exhilarating to belong to a "go-ahead" Church, even if the Vicar does spend more time on buildings than on souls. Not many people will sense the lack of spiritual nourishment and most will be ready to have substituted for it a round of tireless parochial activities. Perhaps Solomon's kingdom might usefully be seen as a picture of a highly organised Church—tip-top building, tip-top music, tip-top weekly programmes. All the important Churchmen are invited to preach at this Church, and in the midst of it all is the Vicar, its creator, tireless and inaccessible. Succeeding generations may even look back with pride—"Those were the days!"

Succeeding generations certainly looked back to Solomon. Foreign embassies coming and going, even a queen from Ethiopia. Remember the chariots! Horses, prancing horses! with royal stables at Megiddo! Israel's king recognised by all the great nations that surrounded her. And to crown all, the Temple—superb, costly, ornate. There was the impressive dedication with an impressive dedication prayer, composed for the occasion. Rivers of blood shed in sacrifice as became a king wishing to impress (I Kings 8, v. 63). Who shall say what genuine religious feeling was not inspired? Even in the heart of the king himself, set as he was in the midst of this stage of his own creating? What a "build-up"! What a triumph for the externals of leadership! Here is a man who has succeeded in that to which he has set his hand. David was astute; Solomon must build a reputation for wisdom. David was the Sweet Psalmist of Israel; Solomon must issue proverbs by thousands and songs by hundreds. David was pious, he danced before the Ark; Solomon must abound in every kind of dazzling religious spectacle. Bigger and better—this is Solomon. Even David's large-heartedness must be puffed out to be a large-mindedness that found room for heathen divinities within Jerusalem itself, the heathen divinities being those Solomon's wives worshipped (I Kings, 11, v. 7). And if Solomon was less intense and ungovernable in his passions than was David, he could at least impress with the size of his harem, seven hundred wives and three hundred concubines!—or should it be seventy (David had sixteen). It at least gave him a name for virility. What a man! It made people think there was something under the padding and stiffening. But the fact remains, that as far as we know he only produced one son.

* * *

Now we look at the reverse side of the picture. Like all excessive building in the ancient world it rested on a basis of slave labour. One month out of every three, men were compelled to labour in the forests of Lebanon felling trees for the building programme. There was a labour conscript force of ten thousand men over which was a grand taskmaster called Adoniram (I Kings 5, v. 13). In addition there were seventy thousand burden bearers and eighty thousand quarrymen. These laboured in slave conditions under three thousand and six hundred Israelite officers. The trees provided by Hiram, King of Tyre, from the forests of Lebanon were dragged overland to the sea, lashed into huge rafts, floated one hundred miles down by the coast, finally to be broken up and dragged overland once more, up to the mountain range upon which Jerusalem stood. Meanwhile the quarrymen toiled in dark subterranean passages pouring out their life's strength in putrid atmosphere to provide the stone to match the timber.

Throughout these years Jerusalem must have provided a sorry sight from the human angle. Always and everywhere, gangs of men and yet more gangs, cursing, sweating, dying, and always the taskmaster ready with his whip and rod. If the Hebrew levies bled, how the Canaanite levies must have bled! And every drop of blood squeezed so that Solomon's God might dwell in a house of Solomon's building, and Solomon himself, his wives and his government dwell in dazzling magnificence. Surely if any buildings were cursed, these (so elaborately described in six chapters of the First Book of Kings) must have been cursed as no other buildings since the days of the erection of the pyramids. And the root cause of all this pile of human misery was Solomon's desire to build a house for God's glory—or was it a house for God for Solomon's glory?

There is something wrong at the root with a religion which does not "do justly, love mercy and walk humbly with its God" (Micah 6, v. 8). And who knows if Micah and all the prophets did not read this lesson first in reading of King Solomon. Genuine religion and social injustice can never march together, which means that the sweated labour of England in the nineteenth century no more commends the religion of that era than did the sweated labour of King Solomon's reign. Neither of course is social justice a substitute for religion. Perhaps this is a lesson that needs to be learned in mid-twentieth century England. But of all religious men who grind down the underdog, Solomon is the father. Such men have fallen a prey to riches which tend to make for hardness of face and insensitivity of soul—"How hard is it for them that trust in riches to enter into the Kingdom of God!" (Mark 10, v. 24). The practical safeguard for the rich is tenderheartedness and generosity. These for their own soul's sake they should cultivate. But Solomon jeopardised his soul when in his prosperity he became cruel.

The truth about Solomon did not altogether appear till he was dead. This is often the case. Then it was divulged how he had chastised the people with whips (I Kings 12, v. 11). Even those who had ruled with Solomon saw the folly of his policy, so that we ought to speak not of the wisdom of Solomon but of the folly of Solomon. It was folly to bleed white a newly established kingdom in order to contribute to the king's "build-up". It was folly to police a people (not long since independent tribes) with bureaucrats, tax-gatherers and professional soldiers, some of whom were foreigners. It was folly to erect a Temple which could be little more than a royal chapel situated as it was next to the king's palace and patrolled by a Praetorian Guard in which were uncircumcised Philistines. It was folly to subdivide the kingdom along lines other than the old tribal divisions for the sake of greater efficiency. It was folly for the State to meddle in the affairs of the Church and for Solomon to depose the old priestly line of Eli and appoint a new priest in the person of Zadok.

Not that all these changes were complete innovations in Solomon's time; their roots lay in the kingdom which David had established. Moreover, some of the changes were inevitable in a people that was moving to a position of greater importance among the surrounding nations. But elevation in life calls for greater spiritual awareness, and in this Solomon gave no lead. This is an important point. To live the godly life amidst wealth and power is not easier than amidst poverty and lowliness, but it is no less necessary. It needs both grace and capacity to achieve it. Unfortunately Solomon lacked both. That was his tragedy. A little man set on a big stage. A round peg in a square hole. And he cut the hole himself and lined it all with gold. . . .

* * *

Can you blame Solomon? What shall a man do who finds himself in the seat of greatness but lacks true greatness in himself? He should accept himself. He should not pad himself and puff himself. He should seek a reputation for large-heartedness and kindness; men will forgive him much if he shows these virtues. And the irony of the situation is that Solomon did begin that way. To Adonijah and Shimei he displayed a commendable clemency. Then he began to strut. But how hardly shall they that strut enter into the kingdom of God. Even their crackling robes look mean and tawdry, or, as Jesus remarked, holding in his hand a flower of the field: "Even Solomon in all his glory was not arrayed like one of these."

II. The Servant of God: Four Studies on "The Servant Songs" of Isaiah

1. THE SERVANT'S BEARING

I MUST apologise for beginning my four addresses technically, that is to say, I apologise for beginning with references to technical points on Old Testament scholarship. But how else can I begin? My addresses are four expositions of the four Servant Songs of Isaiah, and they bristle with problems of literary criticism. It may be, however, that, with a specialised audience such as this, people who have been trained and set apart for Christian work, the handicap of this approach is slight. The handicap indeed might be greater if I did *not* begin in such a fashion, for then you might imagine that I was either unaware of, or lightly regarded, these problems, and neither would be true. More than that, my purpose would be defeated, for this is my purpose—to try to cause us to hear in the reading of these scriptures some Word of God addressed to ourselves; and such religious reading of the Bible can become fanciful unless based on reasonable exegesis, which means paying attention to critical problems.

The Gordian knot in these Servant Songs is the identity of the servant. We cannot by-pass this. Is the servant a person or a personification? Is he part of Israel; all Israel; or the ideal Israel? Is he someone who has already existed; or is he still to come? These are real difficulties, and no solution of them is without problems remaining.

The interpretation I shall follow in these expositions is that the identity of the servant was not clear in the mind of the writer. And I shall take it that the author of the Songs is the same as the author of the context in which they are set. At times I think the author conceived of Israel in whole or in part as the servant of God. At other times I think he conceived of him as a *historical figure*, in particular, Cyrus. But when he saw the failure of both Israel and individual saviours to redeem mankind, and especially when he saw the failure of Cyrus, the Lord's Anointed, his mind was driven by his faith up and out to the conviction that God would not finally desert his people; and this made him delineate what the pattern of God's true servant would be. That pattern is what we have in the Servant Songs. It is the subject of our studies in these four addresses.

But we are not to reckon that this pattern represents "an ideal". The author confidently expected the pattern some day to appear embodied. And Christians believe that this has happened. Jesus is the pattern in human flesh. The Servant Songs represent, therefore, the most mature thought of the Old Testament. No wonder there is no subsequent reference to them in Old Testament literature. The fact is they were not understood till Jesus understood them, and he understood them of himself. Maybe, in the economy of God, they were originally uttered for his sake who should come after. Who shall say? In any case, Jesus fulfilled them. That is to say, he filled them out with meaning. But he did not exhaust them. He left the pattern for his servants down through the ages to fill out. This, be it noted, is our apology for applying these scriptures to ourselves.

Where are these Servant Songs to be found? They are in Isaiah 42, vv. 1-4; 49, vv. 1-6; 50, vv. 4-9; 52, v. 13-53, v. 12. These are the usual delineaments. To them we shall attach four titles—The Servant's Bearing; The Servant's Equipment; The Servant's Experience; and The Suffering Servant.

We begin with the Servant's Bearing and the reading of the first Servant Song and following verses:

> Behold my servant, whom I uphold; my chosen, in whom my soul delighteth: I have put my spirit upon him; he shall bring forth judgment to the Gentiles. He shall not cry, nor lift up, nor cause his voice to be heard in the street. A bruised reed shall he not break, and the smoking flax shall he not quench: he shall bring forth judgment in truth. He shall not fail nor be

discouraged, till he have set judgment in the earth; and the isles shall wait for his law.

Thus saith God the Lord, he that created the heavens, and stretched them forth; he that spread abroad the earth and that which cometh out of it; he that giveth breath unto the people upon it, and spirit to them that walk therein: I the Lord have called thee in righteousness, and will hold thine hand, and will keep thee, and give thee for a covenant of the people, for a light of the Gentiles; to open the blind eyes, to bring out the prisoners from the dungeon, and them that sit in darkness out of the prison house. I am the Lord; that is my name; and my glory will I not give to another, neither my praise unto graven images. Behold, the former things are come to pass, and new things do I declare: before they spring forth I tell you of them.

"Behold my servant" (v. 1). God is the exhibitor. It is as if a stage is set and God draws the curtain to display his own player. He *is* God's player, because without God he would not be there. He is upheld by God; he is chosen by God; he enjoys God's delight, and he is endowed with God's spirit. No wonder this player upon God's stage is not simply "*a* servant" but "*my* servant". He is God's, and without God he would be performing no function at all.

"Behold my servant, whom I uphold; my chosen, in whom my soul delighteth: I have put my spirit upon him;"

But what is his function? It is "to bring forth judgment to the Gentiles" (v. 1b); or, to re-translate the Hebrew, "He shall carry true religion to the peoples." The significant word here is "mishpat". In this context it does not refer to a sentence in a law court, nor is it mere piety; "mishpat" is "right living", as witness Deuteronomy 32, v. 4:

> The rock, his work is perfect;
> For all his ways are *judgment* (i.e., *right*, "mishpat")
> A God of faithfulness and without iniquity,
> Just and right is he.

The function of God's servant then is to carry God's right way of living to the nations or "outsiders". His function is evangelism.

But how shall he perform it? This is what interests us. And the answer is arresting. "He shall not cry, nor lift up, nor cause his voice to be heard in the street" (v. 2).

This quiescence is arresting on account of the power behind the servant. The power is stupendous. It is no less than the power of God himself. And God (so to speak) draws back the curtain to exhibit his servant with a flourish; but that servant does "not cry, nor lift up, nor cause his voice to be heard in the street".

What does this mean? It cannot mean that no attention is to be given to words and language in the carrying out of God's commission. Few writers, if any, stress more than the author of these chapters of Isaiah the power of the spoken word. "Call", "utter", "declare", "sing aloud"—these are frequent expressions. And where will a greater encouragement to the exercise of oratory in the ministry be found than in Isaiah 40, v. 9:

> O thou that tellest good tidings to Jerusalem,
> Lift up thy voice with strength; lift it up, be not afraid;
> Say unto the cities of Judah,
> Behold, your God!

But there is a difference here. In Isaiah 40, v. 3, the word is the deep and sonorous "Kara"; it is the call of the watchman. Here, however, the word is ugly. It is used in Deuteronomy 22, v. 24, of the scream of a raped woman, and in Judges 4, v. 3, of the terror of an overwhelming army, and in Job 19, v. 7, of Job in the agony of his bodily pain and mental anguish. The word is "Ssaak". It is a hissing word, smacking of bitterest onslaught. This is not the manner of speaking God's servant employs.

What we have in Isaiah 42, v. 2, therefore is no disparagement of preaching in the ministry, nor any warrant for lack of animation in preaching (a deadly sin in the pulpit), nor for carelessness in the selection of words. On the contrary, the lower the educational level of the congregation, the greater should be the care and the greater is the opportunity for exercise of skill. Jesus with his parabolic method is the guide. No, Isaiah 42, v. 2, does not eliminate the technique of public speaking—it describes the manner of the speaker, or, in the words of the title of this Bible reading, "the bearing of God's servant".

Apparently there is a worldly manner of speaking, and there is a godly manner of speaking. Of the former, dictators, conquerors and tyrants have shown themselves conspicuous exponents, and it may be that Cyrus was the example of the times to which these scriptures refer. There is power in such speech. And it still exists. The mid-twentieth century with its films, strip-cartoons and television *may* be described as the age of pictures; but the visual image has not ousted the power of the spoken word, nor ever will—for it is elemental, and because it is so, there is a right and a wrong way to use it.

God's servant, therefore, uses speech the right way. He makes no use of vituperation; he does not coerce; he is never "loud"; neither does he advertise himself (G. A. Smith). And if he did, God would not own him, for the servant whom God acknowledges, upholds, takes pleasure in and equips does "not cry, nor lift up, nor cause his voice to be heard in the street."

*   *   *

Now those who hear God's servant speak will expect a tenderness in his pastoral care, and they will not be disappointed. "A bruised reed shall he not break, and the smoking flax shall he not quench" (v. 3).

From time to time it is salutary for the Christian minister to ask himself what he imagines himself to be doing in his ministry. Is he expunging from the minds of the ignorant religious rubbish of which its possessor should be ashamed? —and a strange assortment of theological ideas is frequently harboured by many devout. Is he rebuking the foolish? Converting the sinner? Teaching the teachable? Uplifting the sordid? Guiding the perplexed? Whatever he is doing, or reckoning himself to be doing, of the divinely acknowledged servant of God, it stands written: "A bruised reed shall he not break, and the smoking flax shall he not quench."

And this tenderness will especially characterise his touch of those who would cry with the Psalmist: "All thy waves and storms have gone over me." In any ministry that is Christian, there is no lack of people whose greatest need is comfort—
—and not only the sick, the bereaved, and the anxious; but those whose constant dilemma in life, particularly in business enterprise, is to know how to choose between varying shades of grey in the moral sphere. Problems do not often conveniently present themselves in terms of black and white. Did they so appear, to walk the way of uprightness would only lightly furrow the brow. But in a world where so much is tainted, those who fall need comfort even in the midst of reproof. And this the true servant of God will minister.

"A bruised reed shall he not break, and the smoking flax shall he not quench." We should notice the description that is given here of the Goyim or far-off peoples—they are broken reeds and dimly burning wicks (R.V.Marg.). For all that the doctrine of total depravity seems on the surface to say, we should not let it say what the Reformers did not intend it to say: the truth is, even unregenerate men have some part light. The Christian minister never ministers to people in whom is no goodness to which an appeal can be made. Jesus found goodness in a woman divorced five times (John 4, v. 18), and in a man deeply involved in financial trickery (Luke 19, v. 5). What shall be the bearing of the parish priest towards the non-churchgoing mother who brings her child for baptism? How shall he conduct himself towards the lapsed communicant? The true minister has eyes only for a dimly burning wick. This he cups his hand around, protecting it from draughts, nursing it gently, risking everything lest he should extinguish it, and never, even in the last resort, treading upon it.

There is a warning against clumsiness in St. Matthew 18, v. 6, couched in the strongest terms, and they are the more striking since they are the recorded words of Jesus: "Whoso shall cause one of these little ones which believe on me to stumble, it is profitable for him that a great mill-stone should be hanged about his neck and that he should be sunk in the depth of the sea." The gentleness of the servant's bearing is not, therefore, an extra gift adding charm where it occurs; it is an essential attitude he lacks at his own peril, and not only his own—such is the seriousness of the matter, he lacks it at the peril of those to whom he ministers. Quench by clumsiness the dimly burning wick and the servant has lost his man.

"The dimly burning wick he will not extinguish." But this is not the whole of the servant's ministry. He is concerned not only not to destroy, he is concerned to save. So v. 3b, "He shall bring forth judgment in truth," which (under the guidance of Delitzsch) might be translated, "He will cause right conduct (mishpat) to develop in acts of integrity and truth."

* * *

At this point there follows an encouragement. He who ministers gently in the fashion of God's servant, though he handles broken reeds, does not break himself. Verse 4 reads (R.V.), "He shall not fail, nor be discouraged till he have set judgment in the earth; and the isles shall wait for his law." The word translated "fail" is the same as that used to describe the wick as "dimly burning". Similarly, the words "be discouraged" are the same as those used to describe the reed as "broken". Verse 4 might therefore read, "He shall not burn dimly, nor shall he break . . ." This then is the encouragement, that the minister with the bearing of God's servant in the ministry will never become like those dimly burning wicks and bruised reeds to whom he ministers. And to the pastor in the heat and burden of the day, this is consolation indeed, for nothing haunts him so much as the spectre of breaking and failing. But not only does he not break, he brings his ministry to a successful conclusion (v. 4b)—he sets up the right (mishpat) in the earth and people afar off, even the most unlikely people (i.e., the isles) will long for God's instruction (i.e., law—torah). Thus, the servant by his bearing

makes God's way of right (mishpat) attractive, his gentleness
is the secret of his success.

* * *

Strictly speaking, the remaining five verses form no part of
the Servant Song, but they are closely allied. God who has
been speaking *about* his servant now *addresses* his servant
(vv. 5-9). It is an exhortation to confidence in the ministry.
It is a reminder that behind the gentle servant there stands
the creator God.

"Thus saith God the Lord, he that created the heavens,
and stretched them forth; he that spread abroad the earth and
that which cometh out of it; he that giveth breath unto the
people upon it, and spirit to them that walk therein: I the
Lord have called thee in righteousness, and will hold thine
hand, and will keep thee, and give thee for a covenant of the
people, for a light of the Gentiles" (vv. 5, 6).

And the purpose of this divinely called, sustained and
formed ministry is to open the blind eyes (v. 7). If one
among us has ever attempted to minister to a man suffering
from some affection of the eyes, he will know how gently
he must needs touch them and how patiently he must wait
till the bandages can permanently be removed.

"To open the blind eyes, to bring out the prisoners from
the dungeon, and them that sit in darkness out of the prison
house" (v. 7). Only those who have actually met discharged
prisoners on the morning of their discharge at the prison
gates can tell of the careful handling required. But it can be
left to the imagination how utterly essential was a guiding
hand to the prisoner released from the blackness of an
oriental gaol out into the glare of the eastern sun. But all these
pictures only reinforce the lesson already taught—God's
servant must deal gently. Yet it will be a successful ministry.
To this God pledges his name and his honour; neither will
he for ever allow that which rightly belongs to him to be
transferred to the sham gods of money, pleasure, fame or
whatever are the stars which for the time attract.

Verse 8, "I am the Lord; that is my name: and my glory

will I not give to another, neither my praise unto graven images."

This is God's work in which God's servant is engaged, the God who in history wrought the redemption of his people. This the prophet foretells: "Behold, the former things are come to pass, and new things do I declare: before they spring forth I tell you of them" (v. 9).

* * *

How shall we sum up this first Servant Song? By reminding ourselves that, uninformed by this scripture, we might have already built up our image of God's successful servant. He would be athletic, efficient, eloquent, and scholarly; but over against whatever advantage each or all of these might constitute, the first Servant Song for all its critical problems points to this as characteristic and essential: "He shall not cry, nor lift up, nor cause his voice to be heard in the street. A bruised reed shall he not break, and the smoking flax shall he not quench."

This is the bearing of God's Servant, and from St. Matthew's quotation of it in Chapter 12, vv. 17-21, we may gather that the early Church recognised this pattern supremely in Jesus. And it is his servant we claim to be. . . .

2. THE SERVANT'S EQUIPMENT

Listen, O isles, unto me; and hearken, ye peoples from far: the Lord hath called me from the womb; from the bowels of my mother hath he made mention of my name: and he hath made my mouth like a sharp sword, in the shadow of his hand hath he hid me; and he hath made me a polished shaft, in his quiver hath he kept me close: and he said unto me, Thou art my servant; Israel, in whom I will be glorified. But I said, I have laboured in vain, I have spent my strength for nought and vanity: yet surely my judgment is with the Lord, and my recompense with my God. And now saith the Lord that formed me from the womb to be his servant, to bring Jacob again to him, and that Israel be gathered unto him (for I am honourable in the eyes of the Lord, and my God is become my strength): yea, he saith, It is too light a thing that thou shouldest be my servant to raise up the tribes of Jacob, and to restore the preserved of Israel: I will also give thee for a light to the Gentiles, that thou mayest be my salvation unto the end of the earth.

Thus saith the Lord, the redeemer of Israel, and his Holy One, to him whom man despiseth, to him whom the nation abhorreth, to a servant of rulers: Kings shall see and arise; princes, and they shall worship; because of the Lord that is faithful, even the Holy One of Israel, who hath chosen thee. Thus saith the Lord, In an acceptable time have I answered thee, and in a day of salvation have I helped thee; and I will preserve thee, and give thee for a covenant of the people, to raise up the land, to make them inherit the desolate heritages; saying to them that are bound, Go forth; to them that are in darkness, Shew yourselves. They shall feed in the ways, and on all bare heights shall be their pasture. They shall not hunger nor thirst; neither shall the heat nor sun smite them: for he that hath mercy on them shall lead them, even by the springs of water shall he guide them. And I will make all my mountains a way, and my high ways shall be exalted. Lo, these shall come from far: and, lo, these from the north and from the west; and these from the land of Sinim. Sing, O heavens; and be joyful, O earth; and break forth into singing, O mountains: for the Lord hath comforted his people, and will have compassion upon his afflicted.

SECOND SERVANT SONG

IN our study of the first Servant Song, we noticed that God drew back the curtain of his stage to reveal and describe his own servant fitted for his work. In this second study, we hear that servant speaking for himself:—"Listen, O isles, unto me; and hearken, ye peoples from far:" (v. 1a). That it is the servant speaking is clear from v. 3: "And he said unto me, Thou art my servant; Israel, in whom I will be glorified."

It is tempting because in v. 3 the servant seems to be identified as Israel to discuss this identification, but such would be contrary to our purpose in these expositions. Suffice it to indicate that the servant cannot without more ado be identified as Israel in spite of v. 3 for the simple reason that v. 5 indicates Israel as the *object* of the servant's restoring work. We shall therefore continue to examine the characteristics of the servant; and if we apply them to ourselves, we shall receive at least no discouragement from v. 1b which uses phraseology too strong not to be applicable to an individual: "The Lord hath called me from the womb; from the bowels of my mother hath he made mention of my name."

"The Lord hath called me." Notice first this reference to the call. It places this nameless servant of God in the category of the named servants of God in holy scripture—Moses (Exodus 3, v. 4), Samuel (I Samuel 3, v. 4), Amos (Amos 7, v. 15), Isaiah (Isaiah 6, v. 8), Jeremiah (Jeremiah 1, v. 4). Or, as we should prefer to express the case, these named servants belong to the category of the nameless servant, for *he* presents the pattern. We should observe too the stress laid on the prevenient grace of God. The servant is not God's from the time of his *response* to the call. Moses was not God's servant only from the day of the burning bush in the desert (Exodus 3, v. 4). Neither does God own us *on account of* our response. He chooses us before we choose him (John 15, v. 16). And the choice is not for merit in us, but on account of God's own redeeming love (Deuteronomy 7, vv. 7, 8).

All this is theocentric thinking. Before the servant is, God is. He exists in an eternal present. He knows what the servant will be and how he will respond while he is yet in his embryonic stage; and so much does he behold even then a particular person, he is given a name. "The Lord hath called me from the womb; from the bowels of my mother hath he made mention of my name." Thus the whole movement of the servant's life is embedded in divine Grace.

This is important. It is important because a sense of God's choice and God's call has always been a source of confidence to God's servants. Far from robbing a man of personal initiative, it sets it free for exercise. Thus Amos, instead of fearing Amaziah, pursued his prophesying under the inspiration provided by the memory of his call—"I was no prophet, neither was I a prophet's son; . . . but the Lord took me . . ." (Amos 7, vv. 14, 15). It is indeed to be doubted if ever a powerful ministry was exercised *without* this sense of call. To feel oneself chosen is both to lose a sense of inferiority, and to be freed from the doubts which hinder concentration of energy, and to persist in the face of difficulties. All strength is rooted in God. All effective ministry derives from him. And the emphasis on the call is the more significant since this second Servant Song does not concern the servant's bearing, but the servant's equipment; but no ministry can be considered apart from the call, and there is a sense in which the servant's knowledge of his call is part of his equipment.

* * *

Now when we proceed to enquire with what is the servant to accomplish the ministry, the answer is arresting—it is words. "And he hath made my mouth like a sharp sword" (v. 2a). It is an astonishing fact that the greater part of the Church's resources in men, money and the ministry, its missionary societies, its publications, its secretaries, its organisers, and its buildings exist for the purpose of making it possible for *words* to be spoken. And the sacraments are the words dramatised. And the hospitals, educational facilities, and relief work organised by the Church are the words demonstrated. There can be no doubt—the Church's equipment is words.

Words are effective instruments. Certainly no wise ministry underrates words. The preacher may be astonished at what they effect; direction of life altered, broken homes remade, sinners converted, the sad consoled. He had no other power to effect all this than words! Words spoken from his own mouth! But words can be creative instruments. The army commander uses them to strengthen the morale of his troops before the battle. Even a man patting a dog's head will *speak* to the animal while he stretches forth his hand. Words convey something of the person of the speaker to the one to whom they are addressed. Words are extensions of persons. That is why they are creative. And so we find in the creation account in Genesis, chapter 1: "And God said, let there be ... and it was so"; and in Psalm 33, v. 6: "By the word of the Lord were the heavens made; and all the host of them by the breath of his mouth." And to the creative power of Jesus' words was borne this testimony: "What is this word? For with authority and power he commandeth the unclean spirits, and they come out" (Luke 4, v. 36). And of his own words Jesus said: "The words that I have spoken unto you are spirit, and are life" (John 6, v. 63).

The servant of God must recognise, therefore, that *words* constitute his equipment in his ministry. Rightly used, that is, when the servant does "not cry, nor lift up, nor cause his voice to be heard in the street", they may become *means of grace*. For all their intrinsic majesty, neither Grace, Faith, nor Knowledge, are self-propagating. They need means, and most often words constitute that means. "Faith cometh by hearing, and hearing by the word of Christ" (Romans 10, v. 17). Thus on the lips of the servant of God's choice words become the link between God and man, and they derive their effectiveness from the fact. This has been finely expressed by the Bishop of Bradford in his book on preaching: "Here is the miracle of the divine economy, that between the provision of God and the sin of man stands—the preacher! That between the truth of God and the quest of man stands—the preacher! His the task to link human sin to forgiveness, human need to divine omnipotence, human search to divine revelation." In face of such considerations, the ministry of the word cannot be despised by those who minister.

I know, of course, that undergirding the words there must be the life. The story is told of St. Francis of Assisi beckoning to a young monk and saying, "Let us walk into the town, and there preach to the people." So the old monk and the young one walked from the monastery along a quiet road. As they went, they talked gravely, each sharing spiritual experience with the other. In this manner they came to Assisi, where they strolled through the market place, up and down many a side street, and back to the gateway of the monastery. Only when they were in the shadow of the gateway did the young man remember the errand. "But, Father," he exclaimed in surprise, "we have forgotten to preach to the people!" But, laying his hand on the young man's shoulder and smiling, St. Francis replied, "My son, we have been preaching all the time. As we walked, we were observed. Scraps of our conversation have no doubt been overheard. Our faces and our demeanour have been seen. Thus have we preached, thus delivered our sermon." Then he added, "Remember, my son, it is no use walking to preach if we do not preach as we walk." (From *500 Tales to Tell Again*, by H. L. Gee.)

Before a minister preaches the gospel, he must *live* the gospel. Therefore the first Servant Song describes the servant's *bearing*, and the second the servant's *equipment*. This is the order.

* * *

There is one other consideration on this matter. Speech is an art or a technique. This aspect should be considered *second*, but it should be considered. "He hath made my mouth like a sharp sword . . . he hath made me a polished shaft." The fact should not be overlooked that the greater part of the words of God's forthtellers (prophets) in the Old Testament are written in poetic form. And the Bible as a whole is second to none in the sheer quality of its literature. God's servant should study to be eloquent. He must labour at the choice and arrangement of words. They are his weapons. No soldier engages in battle with a rusty sword or unoiled rifle. Every sermon, every address, every talk should be sharpened and polished. He must never whisper, "This will do."

There is a place for carrying out this preparatory work. It is in solitude alone with God. "And he hath made me a polished shaft, in his quiver hath he kept me close" (v. 2b). The Hebrew for "kept me close" is the ordinary word for "hide", so that we might aptly say every servant of God must have a hidden life. There is great peril in too much activity. A man's ministry does not remain cleaned, polished, and pointed, which is what the Hebrew word means in the phrase "he hath made me a polished shaft", *unless* there is studied quiet. Nor is this the only hidden life a man possesses. There is the sum total of his experiences throughout the years preceding and concurrent with his ministry. This, too, is a hidden life. Outsiders know next to nothing of it, certainly not of his inner reactions, struggles, victories, and defeats. Yet all this is God's cleansing, polishing, and sharpening process. God is all the while preparing his arrow; and he keeps it in his quiver till he requires it. This is the faith in which the servant of God should estimate his life's experiences. They were not haphazard; they were not unfortunate; they need not be finally regrettable. On the contrary, they constituted God's means of preparing his arrow for a service yet to come.

From the first Servant Song, it might be possible to conceive of God's servant as colourless and unconvincing. He does "not cry out, nor lift up, nor cause his voice to be heard in the street". And if he never breaks bruised reeds, nor quenches smoking flax, it might be asked what, if any, success he hopes to achieve. But God's servant is neither weak, nor is he a fool. His words are not raucous, nor are they blunt; but he has words kept in readiness, sharpened words, polished words; and when required, they fly like swift, streamlined, pointed arrows, straight to the mark, straight from God's quiver, accomplishing their purpose with the least possible fuss or commotion, piercing sometimes as may be necessary even the crusts of indifference or evil custom.

The pattern of God's servant presented by these scriptures is thus seen to be one of quiet efficiency. It is to be wondered if it is possible to bear the marks of God's servant in any other fashion than that of quiet efficiency. This *is* the pattern. And here the stress is on efficiency in speech.

* * *

We pass now to a consideration of verse 3: "Thou art my servant; Israel, in whom I will be glorified." The Hebrew word for "glorified" means "adorned" or "made attractive". The meaning, therefore, is that God is made attractive to people through the ministry of his servants. Without them it is improbable that God will be attractive in the eyes of men. God will be feared, ignored, blasphemed, and entreated, but God will not be loved for the beauty of his love unless there are servants on earth to reveal that character. God needs men. God therefore calls servants. And having experienced the love of God in their own call, they are to display that love to the world. So God will "burst forth into splendour" (G. A. Smith) before men. And the medium is *words*.

It may be that this appears an exalted conception of the ministry, perhaps too exalted. It is contrary to experience. The performance of God's service is too often one of failure and disappointment. Is this our reaction? We are not the first so to react. We have it in verse 4: "But I said, I have laboured in vain, I have spent my strength for nought and vanity." But the objector recovered himself. He remembered, as everyone needs to remember, that we see only the surface of results, we do not know the final outcome. We cannot see

123

sub specie aeternitatis. This must be left in the hands of God, and can *safely* be left there. Verse 4b: "Yet surely my judgment is with the Lord, and my recompense with my God," which, following our rendering of "mishpat" (judgment) in the first Servant Song, might be translated: "Yet my right is with the Lord," that is, the right that I did in face of all opposition and difficulty is in God's safe keeping, and my day of reward will appear.

In verses 5 and 6, the servant still speaks, but it is God himself we hear. His words emphasise the magnitude of the servant's task. It is not simply a work of restoration of the lapsed, though this is of first importance, as witness the fact that the servant has been formed by God "to bring Jacob again to him, and that Israel be gathered unto him" (v. 5). But this is not the whole of the servant's task. Pastoral work there must be, but there must also be evangelism. The servant must reach out, and the limits of his out-reachings are far beyond the bounds of nationalities; they are set only by the very ends of the earth (v. 6). "It is too light a thing that thou shouldest be my servant to raise up the tribes of Jacob, and to restore the preserved of Israel: I will also give thee for a light to the Gentiles, that thou mayest be my salvation unto the end of the earth." And so the Church's ministry must be comprehensive. It must be catholic, that is to say, it must guard, it must conserve, it must restore. But it must also be evangelical; it must advance, it must progress, it must incorporate the new. The ideal for God's servant is set by the servant in these Servant Songs. It is to stand in with the old (Jacob) but to reach out to the new (the Gentiles).

* * *

At this point a new but recurring feature of the servant is introduced—he is lowly. A hint of this first occurs in the parenthesis of verse 5, "for I am honourable in the eyes of the Lord, and my God is become my strength". The hint is of dishonour in the eyes of men compensated by honour in the eyes of the Lord, and of human weakness made perfect in God's strength—a theme elaborated by St. Paul in *his* teaching: "But God chose the foolish things of the world, that he might put to shame them that are wise; and God chose the weak things of the world, that he might put to shame the things that are strong; and the base things of the world, and the things that are despised, did God choose, yea and the things that are not, that he might bring to nought the things that are" (I Corinthians 1, vv. 27, 28). It was also tested in his own experience, "And he hath said unto me, My grace is sufficient for thee; for my power is made perfect in weakness . . . for when I am weak, then am I strong" (II Corinthians 12, vv. 9, 10). It is a hint of more to come.

*   *   *

So, strictly speaking, at this point ends the second Servant Song. It consists of chapter 49, vv. 1-6, but we will consider the remainder of the paragraph into which the Song merges.

This hint of lowliness is made definite in verse 7: "Thus saith the Lord, the redeemer of Israel, and his Holy One, to him whom men despiseth, to him whom the nation abhorreth, to a servant of rulers: Kings shall see and arise; princes, and they shall worship; because of the Lord that is faithful, even the Holy One of Israel, who hath chosen thee." The phrase "him whom men despiseth" means "contemptible as regards his soul". This and the words "abhorred by the nations" and "slave of tyrants" stress the lowliness. They almost labour it. They say in effect—the servant may in the eyes of the Lord be *his* servant, but in the eyes of the world he is some heathen tyrant's contemptible, revolting bondslave. The words are as strong as that. Yet the wonder is that God's purpose of redemption for the world is wrought through this lowly servant—"Kings shall see and arise; princes, and they shall worship; because of the Lord that is faithful even the Holy One of Israel, who hath chosen thee" (v. 7b).

Thus there is introduced under the figure of lowliness that feature of the servant which is to become characteristic, namely, suffering. It is introduced again in the third Servant

Song: "I gave my back to the smiters, and my cheeks to them that plucked off the hair . . ." (chapter 50, vv. 6, 7), and developed in the fourth Servant Song: "He was despised, and rejected of men; a man of sorrows, and acquainted with grief" (chapter 53, v. 3).

But the ministry wrought out through lowliness and suffering had God's purpose in it. The servant in his need called out, God answered, and it became a day of salvation (v. 8); and the issue was restoration of property, deliverance from captivity, and the return of the ransomed (vv. 9-12). All this is God's redeeming work in which God's creation is called to play its part. It will be a miraculous deliverance, nothing will be wanting. There will be sustenance at hand for the ransomed even by the wayside and on the rocky roads they must needs traverse (v. 9). And not only food, but drink, real drink. The sun will not deceive them with a mirage (*see* Isaiah 35, v. 7), nor smite them with its scorching heat. The redeemed will find themselves, by God's mercy, beside springs of water, for all the created order is God's; they are God's mountains, and God's highways (v. 11). Men will journey from all directions and from the most distant places conceivable (Sinim, v. 12). So great indeed is the final outcome of God's redeeming work wrought through his lowly servant that no other conclusion is fitting but a poem of praise from the whole created order. . . .

> Sing, O heavens; and be joyful, O earth;
> And break forth into singing, O mountains:
> For the Lord hath comforted his people,
> And will have mercy on his afflicted.   (v. 13)

*   *   *

So ends our study. How shall we summarise the teaching? What lessons are here for the exercise of the Christian ministry? Surely, first and foremost, that God's servant is divinely called to a ministry of preaching, words are his weapons, and words he must learn to wield: through them God is made glorious in the eyes of men.

Secondly, that the ministry must aim not merely at restoration of the lapsed, but at the winning of those completely outside (Goyim).

Thirdly, that lowliness and suffering must be reckoned the characteristic of God's servant, but through this weakness God's strength will be perfected in a rich harvest of redeemed humanity.

Secondly, what the ministry cost, one not merely remembers of the highest, but the of love of those who people can make. (Ch.xxii)

Thirdly, that friendless and suffering souls can read the message it will be prayerful, and believe in presence of the human.

3. THE SERVANT'S EXPERIENCE

Isaiah, Chapter 50, vv. 4-11

The Lord God hath given me the tongue of them that are taught, that I should know how to sustain with words him that is weary: he wakeneth morning by morning, he wakeneth mine ear to hear as they that are taught.

The Lord God hath opened mine ear, and I was not rebellious, neither turned away backward. I gave my back to the smiters, and my cheeks to them that plucked off the hair: I hid not my face from shame and spitting. For the Lord God will help me; therefore have I not been confounded: therefore have I set my face like a flint, and I know that I shall not be ashamed.

He is near that justifieth me; who will contend with me? let us stand up together: who is mine adversary? let him come near to me. Behold, the Lord God will help me; who is he that shall condemn me? behold, they all shall wax old as a garment; the moth shall eat them up.

Who is among you that feareth the Lord, that obeyeth the voice of his servant? he that walketh in darkness, and hath no light, let him trust in the name of the Lord, and stay upon his God. Behold, all ye that kindle a fire, that gird yourselves about with firebrands: walk ye in the flame of your fire, and among the brands that ye have kindled. This shall ye have of mine hand; ye shall lie down in sorrow.

THIRD SERVANT SONG

IN passing to the third Servant Song, we pass to a consideration of the servant's delineaments which we apply only reluctantly to ourselves; and which force us in consequence to turn our minds to some other servant whose work is unique.

What we are touching on is that permanent critical problem for Old Testament scholars, namely the identity of the servant in these scriptures. It is no part of our function in these studies to enter at length into this problem, but we cannot ignore it if we are to penetrate to the heart of these poems as they concern the Church's mission. Suffice it to say, however, that the identity of the servant varies in the four Songs. In the first two, that is, Isaiah 42, vv. 1-4, and 49, vv. 1-6, we shamelessly applied the verses to ourselves. We saw a picture of the servant of God into which we (at least in a measure) would fit. This we can also do for this third Servant Song, but not altogether. Here we begin to pass over to a category which only one servant completely fits, that Servant who alone is able to fill fully (or fulfil)—the category of the servant in the fourth Servant Song—Isaiah 52, v. 13 to 53, v. 12.

Now this passing from God's common servants to God's unique servant, this passing from ourselves who are imperfect servants to Christ who is the perfect servant, is not bewildering but illuminating. As those to whom we minister encounter us, observe us, and hearken to our words, their minds should be carried to One who is greater, of whom indeed we are only the vaguest shadow, but are at least no less. We are ourselves, and Christ is Christ; but in the service of God, that is, when the servant lives out his service, there will be interpenetration, we in Christ and Christ in us.

It may be that the servants of God ought to pray more earnestly for this than for any other gift in the ministry. And the bare thought of it twists itself into a rebuke to the writer as he conceives of his own ministry. How often, how rarely, have those ministered to been caught up by a half-thought that it might perchance be Christ ministering to them in pulpit or at altar. The tragedy is that, unlike the passage of scripture in Isaiah, the identity of God's servant could never be held in question. It is plain Mr. X or Father Y with all his pride, mumbling and clumsiness.

Yet the minister in the Christian ministry is called to be Christ to the people. It is to be doubted if he has any ground for ministry, apart from this. He is to be Christ to the Parochial Church Council (even during sessions). He is to be Christ to the children in the street outside, Christ to the local Borough Council, Christ to the sick. Perhaps the tests for the Christ-bearing success of all our enterprises might be found in the marks we make on all these groups. We are to be Christ when we stand up to preach, Christ when we kneel with the congregation to pray. How often, how rarely, will the parishioners declare of Bishop, Priest or Deacon, "Christ served among us in that man."

Let us, therefore, in this third study be ready to pass from ourselves to the Christ we minister—but we begin with ourselves. We begin with what should be the *experience* of the true servant: "The Lord hath given me the tongue of them that are taught, that I should know how to sustain with words him that is weary: he wakeneth morning by morning, he wakeneth mine ear to hear as they that are taught" (v. 4).

Herein lies a method of teaching of which the Hebrews were masters, and which reached its perfection in Jesus. All the words of Jesus were occasional. It is the besetting sin of too many Christian teachers and preachers that we present abstract doctrine in a vacuum and then are perplexed by the hearers' inattention. If we are to achieve anything in the ministry of teaching, we must begin with the real events which are touching people's lives, and engaging their interest. This is how Jesus taught. It was when there was a dispute about who should be the greatest that Jesus gave his teaching on humility (Mark 9, vv. 33-37; Luke 22, vv. 24-27). It was when a certain lawyer asked, "And who is my neighbour?" that Jesus delivered his immortal words on the nature of true love in the parable of the Good Samaritan (Luke 10, vv. 29-37). Jesus' teaching was occasional. The true servant's teaching is always occasional. "He wakeneth morning by morning, he wakeneth mine ear to hear as they that are taught" (i.e., as disciples: the root of the word means "to chastise", and the reference is to learning the hard way, perhaps on occasions through bitter experience). All the true servant's teaching is what he has made his own by applying

130

to himself; it is part of him, it has in some time past met his own need, and it is stored within himself waiting to be drawn upon as the occasion requires. In the best sense of the word, it is topical, which does not indicate an ephemeral character; on the contrary, it indicates a rich store laid up betimes. This is ministry after the fashion of "the faithful and wise steward whom his lord sets over his household to give them their portion of food in due season" (Luke 12, v. 42). It implies no hand-to-mouth ministry. It implies a rich store from which the occasion determines what shall be served.

"The Lord God hath given me the tongue of them that are taught." Which, being interpreted, means—we can only speak out of the fund of our own spiritual experience. There is a beautiful picture of this in Mark 7, v. 32ff., "And they bring unto him one that was deaf and had an impediment in his speech"—a representation doubtless of more than one Christian disciple of ancient or modern times—" And they beseech him to lay his hand upon him. And he took him aside from the multitude privately, and put his fingers into his ears; and he spat and touched his tongue; and looking up to heaven, he sighed, and saith unto him, Ephphatha, that is, Be opened. And his ears were opened and the bond of his tongue was loosed, and he spake plain." No servant of God will "speak plain" in his ministry unless first Christ has "opened his ears". We have to hear, we have to be taught before we can teach. And for this reason—no Christian ministry teaches merely so that his hearers' fund of knowledge shall be increased; the task is much more delicate. It is to "know how to sustain with words him that is weary" (v. 4). The remarkable fact is that words are capable of such action, it can only be that words, as has already been noticed, become the links between God and man; they become the vehicle for the outgrowing and inflowing of *God's* sustaining power. That is why they need not be strident, but gentle—their strength does not lie in themselves. . . .

At this point we begin to pass to descriptions of the servant which we are reluctant to apply to ourselves, and perhaps in honesty cannot. They mark out not the manner of *our* ministry but the person of him who is the *subject* of our ministry. We begin, in fact, to see the suffering servant. We begin to see the teacher as a martyr. "The Lord God hath opened mine ear, and I was not rebellious, neither turned away backward. I gave my back to the smiters, and my cheeks to them that plucked off the hair: I hid not my face from shame and spitting."

There will be difficulties encountered in any Christian ministry, perhaps even suffering, certainly some ostracism, sufficient at least to remind us that it is in the steps of a crucified Saviour that we walk—but of very few will the descriptions given here be warranted. "I gave my back to the smiters, and my cheeks to them that plucked off the hair."

Yet whatever the trials encountered, it is in the confidence of v. 7 and the nature of v. 7 that we must proceed: "For the Lord God will help me; therefore have I not been confounded: therefore have I set my face like a flint, and I know that I shall not be ashamed."

There has to be a certain quality of toughness in the ministry. "Suffer hardship with me, as a good soldier of Jesus Christ" was the advice to Timothy (II Timothy 2, v. 3). God's servant must stand up and be a man, but the ultimate ground of his confidence is not in himself, but in the fact that he is God's servant, and no adversary of God can outlast him, decay will be the adversary's final portion. "He is near that justifieth me; who will contend with me? Let us stand up together: who is mine adversary? Let him come near to me" (v. 8). "Behold, the Lord God will help me; who is he that shall condemn me? Behold, they all shall wax old as a garment; the moth shall eat them up" (v. 9).

G. A. Smith (*The Book of Isaiah*, Vol. II, p. 331) notices why it is the servant receives such violent treatment. It is because he uses words. It is the teacher who hears God's words (v. 4) and is not disobedient to proclaim them (v. 5) who suffers such vicious treatment. Surely it is impossible in the face of these considerations to count words or the ministry of preaching insipid! Men are incensed by words (prophecy)

132

because words can be God's stinging arrows (chapter 49, v. 2). Jesus suffered shame, scorn and spitting although he had caused the hurt of none, nor was there any likelihood of his being violent. ". . . Are you come out as against a robber with swords and staves to seize me?" he asked of the Temple police in the Garden of Gethsemane. "I sat daily in the temple teaching . . ." (Mark 26, v. 55). But therein lay the danger, he taught, he used words, and words are weapons, they may be God's weapons.

* * *

We leave then this transition servant song in which the servant begins to take on the character, not yet of the vicarious sufferer, but of the martyr-speaker, in order to consider two verses which do not properly belong, indeed whose connection is doubtful—vv. 10 and 11. "Who is among you that feareth the Lord, that obeyeth the voice of his servant? he that walketh in darkness, and hath no light, let him trust in the name of the Lord, and stay upon his God" (v. 10). "Behold, all ye that kindle a fire, that gird yourselves about with firebrands: walk ye in the flame of your fire, and among the brands that ye have kindled. This shall ye have of mine hand; ye shall lie down in sorrow" (v. 11).

Two groups are here—those who obey (v. 10) and those who rebel (v. 11). It may be that with reference to God there are no other groups than these. But the arresting fact is that an obedient God-fearer may find himself "walking in darkness with no light"! No facile view of religion is possible after this. No Christian can take it for granted that his path will continually be flooded with light. It is even apparent from experience that every man must continue "in the dark" concerning the answers to many questions. "What will tomorrow bring forth?" "What is the nature of the eternal world which is all about us but of which we are so little conscious?" "What is God like in himself as distinct from the revealed God?" With regard to these matters, man has never been able to do more than grope in the darkness. God in fact has left him there. And some people there are, possessed of doubts concerning revelation, or suffering, or the turns the wheel of fortune has taken in their own lives, they ask "Can there be a God?" Explanations, even apologetics, lead a little through this darkness, and it is no small part of the ministry of some to offer this guiding hand; but in the end the only real possibility is that enshrined in v. 10b: "Let him trust in the name of the Lord, and stay upon his God." This is nowhere brought out so clearly as in the case of John the Baptist in the prison of Machærus and the darkness of doubt (Matthew 11, 2-5). There we find even the forerunner of Jesus doubting the identity of him he heralded. Did this come about because John found Jesus' methods of working unexpected: he did not see Jesus "burning up the chaff with unquenchable fire" (Luke 3, v. 17)? Was it because Jesus performed miracles of healing upon sufferers with obstinate diseases, and yet made no attempt to save him (John) from prison? But whatever the reason, John the Baptist was in the darkness of bewilderment, and Jesus did nothing for him but encourage him to hold on still in the darkness without stumbling. "Go your way and tell John the things which you do hear and see: the blind receive their sight, and the lame walk, the lepers are cleansed, and the deaf hear, and the dead are raised up and the poor have good tidings preached to them. And blessed is he, whosoever shall find none occasion of stumbling in me" (Matthew 11, vv. 4-6). Jesus in fact said what Isaiah wrote. "Who is among you that feareth the Lord, that obeyeth the voice of his servant? he that walketh in darkness and hath no light, let him trust in the name of the Lord and stay upon his God" (chapter 50, v. 10).

* * *

But walking in faith in the darkness is difficult. It is the rub which lies at the heart of the Christian gospel. Men try to break out. They weary of quiescence; they create lights other than the light of the Christian revelation which they declare has failed them. One such light is Marxism, another is Scientific Humanism, and in some quarters—fierce Nationalism. All such are expressions of rebellion against the light religion has not brought or has not obviously brought. And so men kindle their own lights of life, among which must be set Hedonism; but whatever form they may take, of all such the writer of this scripture is despairing; they each will bear the label "the light that failed", and those who sought to walk by them will taste the gall of disappointment, for in face of all life's ultimate questions there is no final alternative apart from faith in God.

"Behold, all ye that kindle a fire, that gird yourselves about with firebrands: walk ye in the flame of your fire, and among the brands that ye have kindled. This shall ye have of mine hand; ye shall lie down in sorrow." Is this driving with the weapon of fear to put our trust in God when the way is dark? But can we avoid it altogether? Of some consequence of action it is only the fool who does not fear. Fear is a necessary alarm bell.

But it may be more salutary to close this reflection on the third Servant Song by reference to the appeal of verses 10 and 11 as a whole. Is any rebellious? Is any *not* rebellious at some part at least of his experience? He should suppress that rebellion. It does not lead to liberty, but rather to the bondage of deeper frustration. There is no other way than to "trust in the name of the Lord, and stay upon his God".

This then is the key to the third Servant Song. In carrying out his ministry, God's servant must expect suffering; but let him neither rebel, nor give way—God's suffering Servant did neither.

4. THE SUFFERING SERVANT

Isaiah, Chapter 52, v. 13-53, v. 12

Behold, my servant shall deal wisely, he shall be exalted and lifted up, and shall be very high. Like as many were astonied at thee (his visage was so marred more than any man, and his form more than the sons of men), so shall he sprinkle many nations; Kings shall shut their mouths at him; for that which had not been told them shall they see; and that which they had not heard shall they understand.

Who hath believed our report? and to whom hath the arm of the Lord been revealed? For he grew up before him as a tender plant, and as a root out of a dry ground: he hath no form nor comeliness; and when we see him, there is no beauty that we should desire him. He was despised, and rejected of men; a man of sorrows, and acquainted with grief: and as one from whom men hide their face he was despised, and we esteemed him not. Surely he hath borne our griefs, and carried our sorrows: yet we did esteem him stricken, smitten of God, and afflicted. But he was wounded for our transgressions, he was bruised for our iniquities: the chastisement of our peace was upon him; and with his stripes we are healed. All we like sheep have gone astray; we have turned every one to his own way; and the Lord hath laid on him the iniquity of us all. He was oppressed, yet he humbled himself and opened not his mouth; as a lamb that is led to the slaughter, and as a sheep that before her shearers is dumb; yea, he opened not his mouth. By oppression and judgment he was taken away; and as for his generation, who among them considered that he was cut off out of the land of the living? for the transgression of my people was he stricken. And they made his grave with the wicked, and with the rich in his death; although he had done no violence, neither was any deceit in his mouth.

*Yet it pleased the Lord to bruise him; he hath put him to
grief: when thou shalt make his soul an offering for sin, he shall
see his seed, he shall prolong his days, and the pleasure of the
Lord shall prosper in his hand. He shall see of the travail of his
soul, and shall be satisfied: by his knowledge shall my righteous
servant justify many: and he shall bear their iniquities. Therefore
will I divide him a portion with the great, and he shall divide
the spoil with the strong because he poured out his soul unto
death, and was numbered with the transgressors: yet he bare the
sin of many, and made intercession for the transgressors.*

FOURTH SERVANT SONG

In passing now to a consideration of this fourth Servant Song,
we pass from a consideration of ourselves in the ministry to
a consideration of him whom we minister. Our warrant for
this transition is the fluidity of the identity of the Servant
in these scriptures, that is to say, the word "servant" does
not always refer to the same person or persons.

The theme of this fourth Servant Song is Suffering—
a theme which began to be introduced in the third Servant
Song. It is a theme which has never ceased to *startle* men
(R.V.Marg.), nor ever ceased to worry them. Sermons on this
subject arrest.

In more unenlightened days than our own, men used to
neglect or even kill the sick. And this had nothing to do with
lack of compassion. They killed the sick in order to avoid the
problem the sick posed. Of this profound disquiet in the face
of illness the restlessness of Job's three friends is witness.
They were disturbed not primarily by his cursings, but by
the fact of his ailing. And for this reason—the disease of Job
(a righteous man) shattered simple theories of the purpose of
men's existence.

This is the bewilderment that lies behind the first verse of
our study. Here was *God's* servant suffering to an excessive
degree. "Like as many were astonied at thee (his visage was
so marred more than any man, and his form more than the
sons of men)" (52, v. 14). The situation was in fact startling—

137

"So shall he startle many nations; Kings shall shut their mouths at him: and that which they had not heard shall they consider" (v. 15 R.V.Marg.).

The elementary view of life is that life should consist of a journey from discomfort to comfort, from pain to pleasure, from want to plenty. Then it would make sense. So doubtless the Hebrews reckoned till they ran through their various saviours who did not finally save, and then they arrived at this *startling* conclusion, that suffering seems embedded in the stuff of the universe. It is not outgrown; neither is it banished; not even by progress. Apparently, man progresses with pain, perhaps by pain. Nor can pain be avoided by sinlessness. This is sufficiently startling to be shocking. But the implication is that, if suffering is fundamental in life's constitution, then even God's Servant, even Messiah, must suffer. So Mark 8, v. 31: "The Son of Man must suffer many things."

To all who cherish the elementary view of life this permanent ministry of suffering is unbelievable: "Who hath believed our report? and to whom hath the arm of the Lord been revealed?" (53, v. 1). To superficial observers not only has such a doctrine no attraction, but neither has the Messiah who embodies it. "For he grew up before him as a tender plant, and as a root out of a dry ground: he hath no form nor comeliness; and when we see him, there is no beauty that we should desire him" (v. 2).

Even the most attractive servant of God would be unattractive if he suffered, unattractive because inimical to straightforward theories of progress. "He was despised and rejected of men, a man of sorrows, and acquainted with grief: and as one from whom men hide their face he was despised, and we esteemed him not" (v. 3). He is in fact repulsive and contemptible.

* * *

But there are other grounds for holding back. Suffering does not automatically redeem. It does not always redeem. Perhaps it does not often redeem. During the Korean war, British troops were astonished to discover the degree of suffering the average Korean would endure without a murmur—physical pain, privation, mental anguish. But the same Korean would be utterly indifferent to the sufferings of his fellows. He would pass a comrade writhing in agony and do nothing. Suffering does not necessarily refine. It may coarsen. This also is why God's servant suffering is startling. Suffering does not necessarily uplift.

Why then *does* God's servant suffer? It cannot be because of his sins. This verse 9 makes plain. He is in fact God's *righteous* servant (v. 11). In any case sin and suffering do not balance each other in life. Some men sin without much suffering. Some men suffer without much sinning. If then God's servant suffers, it may be for some deeper reason than that he is caught in the general human network; it may be that there is a ministry in suffering, and he is accounted worthy to fulfil it.

If such be the case the problem is reversed. It is not why the good man suffers, it is why the bad man suffers. Suffering can do little for the bad man except make him worse. It can make a law-breaker a blasphemer in his dying agony (*see* Luke 23, v. 39); whereas in the case of the good man, suffering can be an effective instrument in raising the standard of life in all who observe him.

*　*　*

It is difficult at this point not to introduce a theological word. Perhaps it is indispensable. It is the word "vicarious". Certainly verse 4 goes straight to its meaning. "Surely he hath borne our griefs and carried our sorrows." From which we conclude that we shall not understand God's servant suffering unless we understand it as vicarious, that is, a ministry of suffering on behalf of others.

We understand this of Christ. There is no man who is a Christian who does not see some glimmer of this truth. But a further question is—Did Christ exhaust this ministry? Is there here still a ministry for God's servant? A ministry for Christ's servants? A ministry for the Church? Apparently there is. St. Paul wrote (Colossians 1, v. 24): "Now I rejoice in my sufferings for your sakes, and fill up on my part that which is lacking of the afflictions of Christ in my flesh for his body's sake, which is the Church."

This is disturbing. And yet it may for some hearer, even in this congregation, illuminate some day of trial. Is some servant of God despairing in his labours? Cast down in his home? Or bewildered in his own personal experience? And does he ask, as well he may, "Why has this thing come to me? Am I perchance out of God's favour?" To whom this scripture might make answer: "No, friend, not out of God's favour, but in God's favour. There is no higher ministry to which a man can be called than the ministry of suffering, vicarious suffering, suffering which is redemptive. Do not be broken by this that has come to you . . . lift up your heart. Maybe God is calling you to help fill up that which is lacking . . ."

* * *

But we pass to a ministry *we* cannot as God's servants fulfil—it is an objective atonement. But it *is* fulfilled. And it implies a uniqueness of ministry, one standing over against the many. "But he was wounded for our transgressions, he was bruised for our iniquities: the chastisement of our peace was upon him; and with his stripes we are healed" (v. 5). And this uniqueness is necessary for a ministry to a humanity interlocked in a sinning network. And this *is* our case. One man sins and another man suffers. No man lives unto himself, and no man sins unto himself. We live each man in relation to his fellow. And so the sins of one cannot be borne away unless the sins of all are borne away. There must be an objective atonement before there can be subjective atonement. This is profound. But the subject is profound. Yet in the familiar words of the Song these depths of thought are plumbed.

All we like sheep have gone astray;
We have turned everyone to his own way;
And the Lord hath laid on him the iniquity of us all.
(v. 6.)

And now our work is clear. We have not only as God's

servants to minister and suffer. This, it is true, will uplift; it may partly redeem; it is a moral redemption, and it works subjectively. But it is not more than this. It does not bear away sin. It could not. Its servants are netted in sinning humanity themselves. They are unworthy and therefore incapable for such a ministry. And so God's Servant suffers for his ministers, suffers, that is, to provide them with a ministry. It is an objective atonement which is indeed experienced subjectively. Let them therefore minister that suffering. Let *us* minister it. It is the least we can do. It is the most we can do.

"The blood of our Lord Jesus Christ which was shed for thee, preserve thy body and soul unto everlasting life."

The Cross therefore must be central. It is central in the sacraments. It must be made central in the ministry of the Word. And, let it be noted, not merely because it is central in Christian orthodoxy, but because it is central in life. Life is produced by way of suffering. It is the stuff of the universe. To make it peripheral is to abandon the key. And here, if anywhere, those polished words, of which the second Servant Song bore testimony, will be required—clumsy handling of this theme will do more to "bruise the broken reed and extinguish the dimly burning wick" than almost any other form of clumsiness.

And the seeming unfairness of life must be touched upon. This is an aspect of experience which has never ceased to trouble. As one woman remarked to me after the war: "I had one son; my neighbour had three. All four boys joined up, my one did not return, her three did. Why? Is there not a God of justice?" Or, as the Psalmist lyrically expressed it: "And why? I was grieved at the wicked: I do also see the ungodly in such prosperity: For they are in no peril of death: but are lusty and strong" (Psalm 73, vv. 3 and 4).

God's most righteous servant tasted unfairness. "He was oppressed, yet he humbled himself and opened not his mouth; as a lamb that is led to the slaughter and as a sheep that before his shearers is dumb; yea, he opened not his mouth.

"By oppression and judgment he was taken away; and as for his generation, who among them considered that he was cut off out of the land of the living? for the transgression of my people was he stricken.

"And they made his grave with the wicked, and with the rich in his death; although he had done no violence, neither was any deceit in his mouth" (vv. 7-9).

This is not foretelling details of the life of Jesus of Nazareth. If it were, it must be counted inaccurate. Although Jesus was silent during part of his trials, he was anything but silent during Passion week; he engaged his enemies in sharpest polemical discourse. Neither could burial in Joseph of Arimathea's tomb be described as burial with the wicked rich. But in seeing through to the bitterness of suffering which God's servant must taste if he were to know its sharpest poignancy, the author of these Servant Songs made the Servant experience unfairness. And because Jesus fulfilled the pattern, he too tasted unfairness. It is not surprising that similarity exists.

On the surface verse 19 is harsh. "Yet it pleased the Lord to bruise him." But the meaning is—in spite of the unfairness of the Servant's suffering, for he was quiet and innocent, God had a purpose in it. The suffering was no miscarriage of justice. And the noteworthy fact about Christ's cross is that it did not cause men to believe in God's *in*justice. Instead, through it they came to believe in God's love. "God was in Christ reconciling the world to himself." It is a grand theme the closing words of the fourth Servant Song feel after. "Yet it pleased the Lord to bruise him; he hath put him to grief" (Hebrew—made him sick).

"When thou shalt make his soul an offering for sin, he shall see his seed, he shall prolong his days, and the pleasure of the Lord shall prosper his hand.

"He shall see of the travail of his soul, and shall be satisfied: by his knowledge shall my righteous servant justify many: and he shall bear their iniquities.

"Therefore will I divide him a portion with the great, and

he shall divide the spoil with the strong; because he poured out his soul unto death, and was numbered with the transgressors: yet he bare the sin of many, and made intercession for the transgressors" (vv. 10-12).

* * *

We return to the beginning, the first Servant Song.

"A bruised reed shall he not break, and the dimly burning wick shall he not quench" (42, v. 3 R.V.Marg.). It is true, the servant of God will not break, but God's righteous Servant (chapter 53, v. 11) *was broken*. The former will not extinguish, but the latter *was extinguished*. "He descended into hell." That is the part of the service of God we shall not experience as he experienced it. But it is an essential part. And no ministry will be effective which does not bear testimony to it in words; in short, we must minister Christ crucified.

* * *

How shall these studies of the Servant Songs be concluded? There is no way but to point to him in whom they are filled full but not exhausted. Christ was gentle. Christ was a polished shaft. He learned of God in the common things of life, using them with a skill beyond compare as he blended them in parable and metaphor to lead men home to God. Above all and through all he tasted death for every man and for all our lesser ministries. His is the service our service represents. We are the servants of him who is "The Servant". It is the suffering, even the broken Christ we minister. And when we do, the words of this unknown author of the Servant Songs find fulfilment:

"He shall see of the travail of his soul, and shall be satisfied: by his knowledge shall my righteous servant justify many."

PART THREE

A COLLECTION OF INDIVIDUAL SERMONS

1. FIRST PRINCIPLES

GENESIS, CHAPTER I, VV. I, 24-27

In the beginning God created the heaven and the earth.

*And God said, Let the earth bring forth the living creature
after its kind, cattle, and creeping thing, and beast of the earth
after its kind: and it was so. And God made the beast of the
earth after its kind, and the cattle after their kind, and every
thing that creepeth upon the ground after its kind: and God saw
that it was good. And God said, Let us make man in our image,
after our likeness: and let them have dominion over the fish of
the sea, and over the fowl of the air, and over the cattle, and
over all the earth, and over every creeping thing that creepeth
upon the earth.*

*And God created man in his own image, in the image of God
created he him; male and female created he them.*

GENESIS 1, v. 1: In the beginning God . . .

I would like you to imagine yourself wandering along the
street and turning over some books in a second-hand book-
shop. And now your eye falls on one entitled *The Lighting of
Houses.* You pick it up and open it. In great detail it discusses
the rival merits of paraffin lamps and candles. It even describes in great detail where they should be set in a house to
give the best effect; and how they should be trimmed.
Wouldn't you smile? And wouldn't you either toss it down on
the pile as useless; or, if you kept it, wouldn't it be solely
for its antiquarian value? After all, we've got beyond the
stage of lamps and candles, anyway for anything but table
decoration.

Now for many people this is the problem of the Bible, or at

least that part of it we are going to consider this morning—
the book of Genesis. It starts by describing the beginnings of
the world in terms no school-boy would recognize. There
is no understanding here of the earth as a globe revolving
round the sun, nor any hint of the most elementary knowledge
of our solar system. Not only is Sir James Jeans more
enlightening on these matters, but even Copernicus who
lived in the fifteenth century.

So what shall we do? Reject the whole Bible because of this
piece of unscientific writing in the first book? Or shall we
preserve it as having antiquarian value?—"This is how people
used to think before the dawn of our scientific era!"

I believe we shall be making a profound mistake if we take
either of these courses. What is more, we shall make the
mistake because we shall be expecting from Genesis what it
cannot be expected to give. We shall in fact be asking the
wrong question. The enquiry to make of the first book of the
Bible is not "What does this piece of writing tell us about
earth's earliest ages?"—the geologists can answer that
question with far greater understanding; the right question
to ask is: "What does this book of Genesis tell us about
God?"

I know of course that the compilers of Genesis, chapter 1
(writing perhaps in the sixth century B.C.), *thought* that they
were giving a true account of the beginnings, or genesis, of
our earth; but it wasn't their *primary* aim to be giving this.
They were out to reveal the revelation of God that they had,
and they did it by using the imperfect scientific thought
forms of their age. That God should allow himself to be made
known to men through such imperfect media is perhaps
surprising, but it is not out of alignment with the revelation
given at Bethlehem through a Baby cradled in straw; in
fact, throughout the Bible God makes himself known to
humble men in humble circumstances. Or to express the
matter bluntly, What was God to do? Wait till men understood Copernican science before he revealed himself as
Creator? The truth is, God has to reveal himself according as
men are able to understand. Theologians call this the principle

148

of divine accommodation. It is everywhere in the Bible, and it stands out prominently on the first page—the book of beginnings, the book of Genesis.

*   *   *

Secondly, the book of Genesis tells us about man; not about man in himself, but man in relation to God. Indeed, this is the profound insight of the book that man cannot be understood *except* in relation to God. Neither Darwin, Nietzsche, Marx, nor Freud therefore hold the key to this interpretation because they always see mankind apart from God. Dig down deep enough into man, they say, and you will find the answer to your problem. But this is what the book of Genesis says: See men *in relation to God*, and you will find the answer to your problems; and it uses an unique expression to describe this insight—it says man is made in God's image.

You see, I believe these early chapters of Genesis are true, not historically true, but mythologically true. I believe they describe in a symbolic way the truth about God and the truth about man, and the relation between them both. And so, when in the first two chapters of Genesis (compiled from two different sources), the author has set out God in relation to man as Creator and created, he goes on to show how unsuccessfully life works out when lived apart from God. Four illustrations of this are given. First, we are shown that not even a perfect environment can make man safe. He fell in a veritable paradise even God had made! (Genesis, chapter 3). Secondly, we are shown that progress in the arts and sciences does not necessarily make for safety. Man certainly progressed, but he progressed in company with sin, and not away from sin—this is the story of Cain and Abel and its sequel (chapter 4). Neither do world calamities teach the world a lesson. After the calamities caused by even a flood of wickedness, evil reasserted itself, yes, even through the family of Noah preserved by the Ark (chapters 6-9). This is knock-out teaching to any facile optimism about the corrective influence of history. And fourthly, life is not made safe by any man-made efforts at collective security; misunderstandings and

149

suspicion result. This is the lesson of the tower of Babel (chapter 11).

Yes, the first eleven chapters of the book of Genesis are depressing, they show so little hope of permanent success in the art of living if man seeks to arrange his life contrary to his nature. He is made in the image of God, and cannot hope for safety if he tries to live as if this were not true.

*　　*　　*

And so we come to the third lesson from this book. It is that the way of faith in God is the principle of safety. But we are not simply told this truth. Neither is it presented in mythological form. We are given four illustrations from history. And for this reason, that man is not simply left to find his own way back into the right relation of safety with God, God takes the initiative. He acts. He does something, in presence of which it is for man to respond, and, when he does, it is an act of faith and this becomes the means of his salvation.

The four illustrations are full of lessons. They are the stories of Abraham, Isaac, Jacob, and Joseph, and they cover the remainder of the book from chapter 12 to chapter 50. Each of these men was different from the others: Abraham was a pioneering type, Isaac was a passive man, Jacob was a schemer, and Joseph was a sufferer. All of which goes to show in the very first book of the Bible that faith is not a matter of temperament, it is a matter of the will. Faith is obeying God and trusting God—and the two cannot be separated—in the circumstances in which we find ourselves.

I would like this to be noted. Sometimes you may be tempted to grow irritated with me. I do not tell you, I *will* not tell you, exactly what you ought to think and what you ought to do. I do not conceive it any preacher's task. My duty is to call your attention to the fact of God within your situation whatever it may be—success, frustration, joy, sorrow, bewilderment, excitement, boredom—*and* to encourage you to faith. It will not be the same call to all types. It will not be the same call in all environments. But if you obey God

and trust God in the circumstances in which you find yourself, it will be a way of safety. It is on the authority of the
gospel of salvation through faith in Christ that I assert it.

The last character in the book of Genesis is Joseph. He
would be a dull reader who did not discern that the com-
piler of Genesis sought to portray him, as far as he could, as
a faultless man, and yet he suffered. That is the great fact
about Joseph. Sold into slavery, misjudged, imprisoned in a
common gaol, bitter sufferings, and with it all, innocence.
But he rose to be Prime Minister, and through years of
famine led his family, Egypt and, in a sense, all the known
world, to safety because all peoples sought the granaries of
the Nile valley stocked through Joseph's policy.

A romantic story? Yes! A treasure for Hebrew parents for
many generations to tell their children after them? Yes! But
is this all? Is it not rather the beginning in the book of
beginnings (Genesis) of the unfolding of that eternal principle
whereby in the economy of God the innocent suffer for the
guilty to win them back to safety? Of course it is true that
interpretation such as this could be dismissed as "reading
back". But the significance of an event is not only the event
itself, but the event "lit up" by subsequent history. Thus
Jesus, God's innocent sufferer who yet saves the world,
lights up Joseph. And in this light we see in Genesis not only
the principle of faith as the way of safety, but God's provision
of a Saviour, a faultless suffering leader.

*   *   *

"In the beginning God." This is the truth to which
Genesis points, not only as a fact in time, but that behind the
created order and behind the existence of the human race,
there stands the everlasting God. We cannot therefore understand the world without God. We cannot therefore understand man without God. To make the attempt is to fail.
But safety there is for all who will grasp it. It lies in the exercise of faith in the God who knows the end from the beginning and the beginning from the end; he has created and he
has provided. So he is our Saviour. . . .

151

2. HOW GOD GIVES

EXODUS, CHAPTER 16, VV. 2-15

And the whole congregation of the children of Israel murmured against Moses and against Aaron in the wilderness: and the children of Israel said unto them, Would that we had died by the hand of the Lord in the land of Egypt, when we sat by the flesh pots, when we did eat bread to the full; for ye have brought us forth into this wilderness, to kill this whole assembly with hunger.

Then said the Lord unto Moses, Behold, I will rain bread from heaven for you: and the people shall go out and gather a day's portion every day, that I may prove them, whether they will walk in my law, or no. And it shall come to pass on the sixth day, that they shall prepare that which they bring in, and it shall be twice as much as they gather daily.

And Moses and Aaron said unto all the children of Israel, At even, then ye shall know that the Lord hath brought you out from the land of Egypt: and in the morning, then ye shall see the glory of the Lord; for that he heareth your murmurings against the Lord: and what are we, that ye murmur against us? And Moses said, This shall be, when the Lord shall give you in the evening flesh to eat, and in the morning bread to the full; for that the Lord heareth your murmurings which ye murmur against him: and what are we? your murmurings are not against us, but against the Lord. And Moses said unto Aaron, Say unto all the congregation of the children of Israel, Come near before the Lord: for he hath heard your murmurings.

And it came to pass, as Aaron spake unto the whole congregation of the children of Israel, that they looked toward the wilderness, and behold, the glory of the Lord appeared in the cloud. And the Lord spake unto Moses, saying, I have heard the murmurings of the children of Israel: speak unto them,

*saying, At even ye shall eat flesh, and in the morning ye shall
be filled with bread; and ye shall know that I am the Lord your
God.*

*And it came to pass at even, that the quails came up, and
covered the camp: and in the morning the dew lay round about
the camp. And when the dew that lay was gone up, behold, upon
the face of the wilderness a small round thing, small as the
hoar frost on the ground. And when the children of Israel saw
it, they said one to another, What is it? For they wist not what
it was. And Moses said unto them, It is the bread which the
Lord hath given you to eat.*

<hr>

EXODUS 16, v. 15: And when the children of
Israel saw it, they said one to another, What is
it? For they wist not what it was. And Moses
said unto them, It is the bread which the Lord
hath given you to eat.

<hr>

ABOUT eight years ago, that is before I came to Kensington,
I was desperately in need of £1400 for my church. We had
committee after committee to try to think how to raise this
money, but all to no avail, it seemed quite beyond our powers.
Then it happened: one morning when things looked most
difficult, I opened one of my letters and inside was a cheque
for just £1400. And you will say, as I said at first, someone
must have heard of the need. But no, the money had been
left in a Will dated ten years previously—so ran the lawyer's
letter. So who will blame me if I called that money "God's
provision"? Manna, pennies from heaven!

And you've had experiences like that—it may not have been
money you needed, but a house, or a flat, or a job, or a friend.
And when the sky seemed most overcast with no possibility
of your need being met, unexpectedly the miracle happened,
your need *was* met—or was it a miracle? Might it not have
been after all a strange coincidence?

I bring to your notice this morning the appointed lesson for this Sunday service—the children of Israel beating their way across the Sinaitic desert after their outbreak from the shackles of Egypt. Day after day they forced their weary limbs over the pitiless wastelands, the sun showing no mercy, the night showing no mercy: heat and cold, hunger and thirst, the whimpers of the children, the moaning of the aged, it was enough to break the stoutest heart. And hearts did break, and voices were uplifted, voices of murmuring: "Would that we had died by the hand of the Lord in the land of Egypt, when we sat by the flesh pots, when we did eat bread to the full."

Have you ever felt like that? Have you ever felt that it would be better to be dead than to go on with life's painful pilgrimage? Oh, we may not often feel like that, but that is how the Israelites felt. . . . And ever since I noted in the lectionary that this was the lesson to be read on the second Sunday after Easter, I've been wondering why—till at last it has dawned on me. Why, of course, as often as not, after some mighty delivering experience like Good Friday and Easter when we touch the peaks of spiritual experience, or when you've given of yourself in some self-spending effort, a dull, plodding, pedestrian period follows. And you start wondering if the spiritual interpretation of life is worth the candle after all. Would it not be better back with the old life; the old world with its old conditions?

And then God provides. It is of his mercy that he provides. It is a case of God accommodating himself to our human frailties, but God *does* this. It is made abundantly plain by the Exodus narrative. We ought of course, all of us, to go on believing in God and trusting in God and obeying his will even when we're exhausted, when everything is against us in life, obedient to the death as Jesus was, South Pole explorers, or Himalayan climbers in the spiritual realm who never turn back. But because we do not all achieve this spiritual heroism, God does not therefore cast us off; he gives bread in the wilderness, manna from heaven.

There is something humiliating about this provision of God. Humiliating as when a boy at school wants to qualify for the First XV and he's not up to it and the captain offers him a place in the Second XV. Humiliating when we want to be first-class believers and God offers us help at a lower level. Humiliating but I suppose comforting as well. God knows our frailties, he knows us through and through, and never asks more than we are able; or as St. Paul put it: "He will not suffer you to be tempted above that ye are able but will with the temptation also provide a way of escape that ye may be able to bear it."

But God's provision is subtle. It is never aimed solely at comfort but also at development. That is why God does not spoon-feed. That is why the Israelites in the wilderness had in the divine economy to go and fetch the food which God provided. And they discovered that it was uncooked. Furthermore, they had to collect it fresh every day.

And this is a point about the manna: "When the children of Israel saw it, they said one to another, What is it? for they wist not what it was." It might have been "MAN", an exudation from local trees. It might have been a dry edible lichen sometimes found on the rocks in the desert. That is to say it was not *obviously* divinely provided at all; it might have been due to natural causes, strange though it appeared.

And so is God's provision normally. That flat, that job, that friend who turned up just when you most needed him— was it a miracle? Or might it not have been after all only a strange coincidence? Or the Resurrection of Christ from the grave? Or the whole corpus of religious experience? Is it of divine origin? Or is it not due perhaps to some natural psychological causes. Professors are not wanting who make this claim.

So you see God's provision is subtle. He meets our need but he requires our effort. It is so because he is concerned with development as well as with comfort. In the presence of his gifts we must make the effort to faith. We must rise up if we would be believers. We must *determine* to accept.

*   *   *

I hope it will not seem out of place if I say that it seems to me a pity our social reformers have not paid more attention to this divine method of giving. I am all for succouring the afflicted, educating the poor, meeting the necessities of strangers; but I do not think we improve people by emphasising comfort. I am told by educationalists (and it does not surprise me) that academic standards are not so high now as when financial grants for students were more difficult to obtain. By all means let help be available for the poor student, but let it be by way of scholarships, plenty of scholarships, graded to various levels. Do not give good things away. Let there be work for them. In the divine economy we have to work *even* for faith.

* * *

I come back to this manna or God's provision for human sustenance. What is it for us? Our Lord left us in no doubt: "I am the bread of life," he said, "Your fathers did eat manna in the wilderness and are dead, I am the living bread: if a man eat of this bread he shall live for ever."

I would like you to see in imagination those Hebrews in the wilderness, each carrying his pot or vessel, some earthen, some golden, it did not matter, but all had to journey daily to collect that manna if they would live at all. And our manna is Christ, we need him, we need to partake of him for spiritual life. And what is your pot, your vessel, which you must bring to gather him? It could be prayer, it could be the sacraments, it could be Bible study, it could be Church fellowship, it could be Church attendance. Note, please note, that all these religious exercises are means to an end, they are not ends in themselves. Their purpose is to enable us to partake of Christ who is our food; without this end they have small justification. Without these means we shall not gather.

I come back to where I began. When we're down, worn out perhaps and frustrated—in surprising ways, God gives us his manna in the wilderness. It is humiliating that we should have arrived at the place of needing it. But if we receive it, receive it in faith as God's provision, making the effort which this reception requires, we do not stay at the humbler level, we rise up, we become integrated persons. Such is God's aim, and such is our opportunity. Remember, manna is never to be despised: and you have some manna in your life now, if you will only look to see it. How can you despise it when Christ called himself by this very name!

3. POSSESSING THE LAND

JOSHUA, CHAPTER I, VV. I-9

Now it came to pass after the death of Moses the servant of the Lord, that the Lord spake unto Joshua the son of Nun, Moses' minister, saying, Moses my servant is dead; now therefore arise, go over this Jordan, thou, and all this people, unto the land which I do give to them, even to the children of Israel. Every place that the sole of your foot shall tread upon, to you have I given it, as I spake unto Moses. From the wilderness, and this Lebanon, even unto the great river, the river Euphrates, all the land of the Hittites, and unto the great sea toward the going down of the sun, shall be your border. There shall not any man be able to stand before thee all the days of thy life: as I was with Moses, so I will be with thee: I will not fail thee, nor forsake thee. Be strong and of a good courage: for thou shalt cause this people to inherit the land which I sware unto their fathers to give them. Only be strong and very courageous, to observe to do according to all the law, which Moses my servant commanded thee: turn not from it to the right hand or to the left, that thou mayest have good success whithersoever thou goest. This book of the law shall not depart out of thy mouth, but thou shalt meditate therein day and night, that thou mayest observe to do according to all that is written therein: for then thou shalt make thy way prosperous, and then thou shalt have good success. Have not I commanded thee? Be strong and of a good courage; be not affrighted, neither be thou dismayed: for the Lord thy God is with thee whithersoever thou goest.

JOSHUA I, v. 2: . . . arise, go over this Jordan,
thou, and all this people, unto the land which I
do give to them . . .

A FEW days ago I stopped in the street to look into someone's front garden. I know I ought not to have done this because people were living in the house and it is unmannerly to stand looking into other people's gardens. But this one was so untidy. And it was only a matter of months since the occupants moved in. And when they did they ripped up all the crazy paving in the garden and engaged a firm to lay a lawn. I expected great things of that lawn. I expected great things of that garden. But now it is covered in weeds and ugly with sycamore seedlings. Clearly they haven't possessed their property, they've only *half* possessed it: much of it is left to lie in unrecovered wildness.

And as I moved on down the street I began to wonder if my *life* was like that. . . . I suppose my thoughts took that turn because I had just been reading Montgomery's memoirs in which he records how he had said of Sir Winston Churchill "he has filled every unforgiving minute with sixty seconds worth of distance run". It is so easy to occupy only a part of our life, so easy to be satisfied with only partial development. We could *do* more, we could *be* more; but we never rise to possess the land.

I would like to speak to you for a few minutes this morning about the book of Joshua which we start to read on the Sunday after Trinity. But I dared not show my hand at first for fear you would be bored. Indeed I'm almost bored myself when I think about this book. It's a heap of literary problems. The old critical approach won't fit, the new critical approach won't fit; the scholars disagree among themselves—Hölscher and Eissfeldt and North—we are not sure *how* this history ran. But there are lessons here, advanced lessons, lessons about occupying the whole of the land which God has given everyone of us.

And what is the land? It is each day, each year, the whole span of our life from cradle to the grave, yes, and that which follows after. Do we occupy it? Do we subdue it? Do we possess it? I think these are the questions to ask this book, and when we do they yield up striking answers.

First, we are not asked to occupy alone. "Now it came to pass after the death of Moses . . . that the Lord spake unto Joshua the son of Nun . . . saying, Moses my servant is dead; now therefore arise, go over this Jordan, thou and all this people, unto the land which I do give them." That is to say, the people were given a leader.

I would like to stress this point. We are not likely to possess the whole of our land unless we follow a leader. We are not likely to make much invasion in the world of spiritual things unless we have our Joshua. And God gives us Joshuas. Do not let us be evasive about that. They may not always be the kind that we should choose. Joshua was no aristocrat. Joshua was no giant. He was neither the son of Moses, nor had he the capacity of Moses. But he had leadership, and like oil in the desert or gold in the Transvaal, you have to take it where you can find it.

I am quite open about this. I am prepared to say in public of myself—if I have entered at all into the fulness of life (and I am sure I still have many miles to go), it is owing to the leadership of four or five that I have tried to follow. One teaches one thing, and another another, and a third something else—shall I ever forget the man who introduced me to music? There are leaders, sufficient God-given leaders, if only we will follow them, and, when we do, we find that we have entered a land we hardly dreamed was there.

* * *

Secondly, from the first chapter of the book of Joshua we find that to occupy the land we need a reinforcing presence. And this is offered us. "As I was with Moses, so I will be with thee . . . be strong and of a good courage . . . for the Lord thy God is with thee whithersoever thou goest."

I wonder how many people there are who, if only they had known this, and believed this, would have lived far richer lives. But we are afraid of new experiences, afraid of new discoveries. And it is all so applicable to the present as we go forward into this atomic age. We *could* hold back, we *could* cry off. And sometimes religious people are the last to want to occupy new ground. And the result is always cramped, restricted living.

I think one of the best examples (that has come my way) of what I speak this morning is a woman who died in Eastbourne not many weeks ago, by name Elise Randall, aged about seventy. She ran a domestic college for girls and had done so for fifty years, building it up from almost nothing. Here was a woman who lived in all the territory of her life, always ready to learn, always moving with the times, always quick to take new people to her heart. And how young people loved her! She lived this book of Joshua; indeed she almost was a kind of Joshua in herself, except that she was very feminine. But she was "strong and of a good courage" believing that God was with her "whithersoever she went".

Christians *ought* to be like that, never dull, never bored, never holding back through fear, for we have a reinforcing presence: "The Lord God is with thee whithersoever thou goest."

* * *

Follow some spiritual guide! Trust in God's presence! Is there any other lesson from this chapter of the book on Joshua? Yes. "This book of the law shall not depart out of thy mouth, but thou shalt meditate therein day and night, that thou mayest observe to do according to all that is written therein: for then thou shalt make thy way prosperous, and then thou shalt have good success."

I expect this verse was added to what is technically called the basic JE strand of history by the Deuteronomic Redactor. But that doesn't make it an untrue insight into life! We shan't fully occupy our lives unless we meditate; or rather, we shall occupy them with many useless things. We must give ourselves time. We must think. We must look where we are going. And if Army Commanders ought to do this, according to Field-Marshal Montgomery, clergy ought to do it, and hard-pressed business men. Meditate! Meditate with the Bible! "This book of the law shall not depart out of thy mouth." Why? Not because it is an arbitrary set of God's eternal wishes, but because it contains the laws of life's effectual working. Do this, "then thou shalt make thy way prosperous, and then thou shalt have good success". Just as the car manufacturers gave me a little book when they delivered me my car: keep these rules, use this oil, "then thou shalt make thy way prosperous and then thou shalt have good success". And do you remember what Jesus said? "If thou wouldest enter into life, keep the Commandments."

* * *

Are you living a full life? Have you entered your land of promise? And as soon as I say this someone wants to rise up and protest: "What would you do if you had my narrow lot? Look at my health! Look at my job! Look at my home! What can *I* do?" Well, my friend, the land of Canaan into which these people went was pretty rough and narrow. It wasn't Egypt, it wasn't Mesopotamia, nor anything like them; but with God's help and their faith—a light shone out from Canaan.

I'm not suggesting that luxury should be yours, ease or even painlessness. What I am saying is that a light could shine from your life and a better light from my life, if only we used to the full the faculties and opportunities God has given us. Enter into life! Difficulties there are. But they are there to be overcome. And when we do overcome them we cause a light to shine.

Did you never read of Rossini, who had to write an opera for a company whose contralto had only one good note to her voice—middle B flat? How easy to complain! How easy to give up! Instead he wrote one of his loveliest pieces, making her sing a recitative on that one note, meanwhile surrounding it with great orchestral music.

And so could you. And so could I. We could enter into life if we trusted God and so gained courage. . . . And I will tell you something more surprising still, we could even enter into the life to come by the same means. I mean we could possess it now. Listen to the words of Christ himself: "He that believeth *hath* eternal life."

And so for all its literary problems, this old book of Joshua still conveys this searching word of God. Have you entered into life? your life, the life which God has given you, with all its rough and pleasant pastures? Have you conquered it, and subdued it? You could if you went forward with faith in God, faith in the prevenient God, faith in the God who always goes before. . . .

4. SPOILED CLAY

JEREMIAH, CHAPTER 18, VV. 1-4

*The word which came to Jeremiah from the Lord, saying,
Arise, and go down to the potter's house, and there I will cause
thee to hear my words.*

*Then I went down to the potter's house, and, behold, he
wrought his work on the wheels. And when the vessel that he
made of the clay was marred in the hand of the potter, he made
it again another vessel, as seemed good to the potter to make it.*

JEREMIAH 18, v. 3: And when the vessel that
he made of the clay was marred in the hand of
the potter, he made it again another vessel.

I WONDER if you have ever "made a mess of things". I don't
mean a complete mess; very few people make a complete
mess of their lives. But I wonder if for you there are some
things about which you have deep regrets. I'm not talking
of some strange experience when I put it like that, am I?
I myself have wished that opportunities could have come my
way which never did. And then there are opportunities
missed. And there are things said which, would to God, we'd
never said. And actions taken—well, looking back they
weren't very wise. And some young people have failed
examinations. And some young man has married the wrong
woman; and some young woman has married the wrong
man—you can tell it now when you see them together. For
some there are incidents for which they were not responsible
—an illness which all but took their strength away; an unhappy

164

home behind them; a make-up which now seems one big bundle of unbound nerve ends. . . .

Am I addressing someone this morning with no regrets of any kind somewhere in the buried past? Then, my friend, I'll leave you behind, just for this morning; but the rest of you I'll take, if you will come, along a narrow street. It is narrow because it is Eastern, but what we are going to see is just the same in principle as in our English potteries—a man sitting at a wheel. And in his hand is clay, and he casts it on the wheel, revolving it with a treadle. Then with his fingers he shapes that clay into a vessel. It stands there before your eyes. You are fascinated, you can scarcely believe your eyes. And there are more finished vessels on the shelf behind. . . . Then the clay splits. Instantly the potter's foot comes off the treadle. The wheel stops. But the potter doesn't throw the clay away. He uses it again. He presses it into a lump. He starts the wheel once more revolving. And now you see *another* vessel taking shape. Made from the same clay, made by the same potter. And you look at all those vessels on the shelf behind, some of which you long to have; and you say to yourself: "Funny thing, they're probably all made from *spoiled* clay."

Do you know who is in our little group? Oh, you wouldn't recognise him if you knew—but it is the prophet Jeremiah. "Then I went down to the potter's house and, behold, he wrought his work upon the wheels." And Jeremiah's head was full of the great mess which his people had made of their history—but not half so full as his heart, for he was a sensitive man. They'd been given a land, but they'd quarrelled over it. They had been granted prophets, men of vision to show God's ways of life and peace; but they only picked up stones to throw at them. Jewry was meant to be a shining example for all the world to see of a nation governed by the laws of righteousness, but she became instead a quarrelsome, bigoted, defeated people, a race without a home.

And with all this in his mind, Jeremiah went down to the potter's home. You know how it is when your mind is filled with something—you don't *see* anything: objects move before

165

you as shapes. And people watching say you have a vacant stare. And that is how Jeremiah stood before the potter's wheel. But the objects clarified. Jeremiah even saw what he was seeing. He saw spoiled clay being remade into beautiful vessels. He saw the potter not casting away the vessel that was marred in his hand but remaking it—and what he saw became to him the very word of God. God does not throw *us* away when we break in his hands upon the turning wheels of life.

Of course, the interpretation was first of all national. It was national for Jeremiah, for he was thinking of his nation. But the word still stands for every one of us. A man may have broken up his marriage—I've had a conversation about that this week. A woman may have failed to hold her children's love; any one of us may have felt the wrong thing, or done the wrong thing, or thought the wrong thing. But whatever it is, whether sin or misfortune, failure to rise to an opportunity, or dogged all the way with crippling ill-health—God never throws us away when we break in his hands upon the turning wheels of life.

*　　*　　*

That's the first fact, and the second is this—God's sovereignty is not rigid. There are some people who have run away with the idea that God has a rigid plan for everyone of us. And they use big words like "determinism" or ordinary words like "fate"; but whatever word they use, they mean the same—God makes out of us what he wants, it's all fixed and settled, we can't do anything about it, we're just clay in the potter's hand. And it isn't true, it isn't one little bit true.

Look at that clay on the floor. The potter does not expect to turn it all to vessels of a certain shape. He makes, and then he makes again upon his potter's wheel. He makes not so much what he wants but what he can. This piece of clay wouldn't make into a jar, so he turns it into a basin. To see the potter doing this is half the fascination.

And don't you see—God is like that. We worry about the

mess we made so long ago; we harp back on that failure; we wring our hands over some misfortune that came just when we were getting going, and those times *were* bad; we did get marred upon the wheels of life. But this is the point—God never casts the clay away because it didn't shape the way he wanted. He simply turns it to another shape.

And someone comes and sits in my study: "If only I hadn't got this nervous make-up." But, my friend, that is the very thing about you that can cause you to become a sensitive leader where you work.

And another is dogged by some indiscretion many years ago. But, my friend, you wouldn't know the exceeding love of God as shewn in his forgiveness were it not for this grave fault. You'd be a Pharisee, you'd be self-righteous, you'd be too proud to live with—or anyway you might be.

And I can see a young medical student dogged with an illness so that he had no chance to specialise but can only be a plain G.P. But you'll go a long way to find a doctor with more tenderness and more tact and more sympathetic insight than he possesses. It is the marring process on the wheels of life that has caused the comely shape that now appears.

* * *

And one more thought before we leave the little street where works the potter on his wheel—we must accept the vessels that we are. I don't mean by this we cannot improve ourselves. I don't mean by this we cannot by the Grace of God achieve a higher standard than once we thought was ever possible; but in the last resort we are as God made us on the wheels of life. And I know no more frustrating attitude than to quarrel with this. It means dropping the "if only's" in our reckoning. *If only* I hadn't been made this way. *If only* this hadn't happened to me when I was young. *If only* I had more skill with my fingers. *If only* I had more brains in my head. But I haven't, and there's an end of the matter. But that doesn't mean God has cast me off from the wheel of life. Nor does it mean a vessel useless and without attraction. We must

167

accept the vessels that we are, and then go forward in this confidence.

May I finish with a story? It comes from one of Schiller's poems. When God made the birds, so the story goes, he gave them plumage gorgeous to behold, and gave them voices entrancing to the ear; but what he didn't give the birds was wings—they had no wings at all. But this is what God did instead. He laid the wings upon the ground. "Take these burdens," he said, "and bear them." And this they did, folding them over their hearts. But presently as time wore on they found the wings had grown fast to their breasts and they could fly. So what they thought were burdens were changed to pinions. Thus Schiller, the German poet, and you smile pityingly at his imagination. But ought you to? And ought I to? When viewed in faith, it is the difficulties of life that raise us higher—or to return where I began, God makes his choicest vessels from spoilt clay.

5. THE HEART OF RELIGION

*Behold, the days come, saith the Lord, that I will make a
new covenant with the House of Israel, and with the house of
Judah: not according to the covenant that I made with their
fathers in the day that I took them by the hand to bring them
out of the land of Egypt: which my covenant they brake, although
I was an husband unto them, saith the Lord:*

*But this is the covenant that I will make with the house of
Israel after those days, saith the Lord: I will put my law in their
inward parts, and in their heart will I write it; and I will be
their God, and they shall be my people: and they shall teach no
more every man his neighbour, and every man his brother,
saying, Know the Lord: for they shall all know me, from the
least of them unto the greatest of them, saith the Lord: for I will
forgive their iniquity, and their sin will I remember no more.*

JEREMIAH 31, v. 33: I will put my law in
their inward parts, and in their heart will I
write it.

I NEVER met my illustrious predecessor in this pulpit, Dr.
James Hannay (alias George Birmingham); nor have
thousands of other people who yet knew him through the
light-hearted novels that streamed from his pen. But
whether you'd met him or merely laughed over his stories,
you *couldn't* know him unless you caught the significance of
the fact that his favourite character in the Bible was Jeremiah
—a man is known by his friends.

Jeremiah was sensitive. I met a man a little time ago, a
clergyman a little older than myself, who confessed he

couldn't take funerals; he wept with the mourners! I know another who was similar, a huge congregation he had, he was Irish, but he likewise couldn't take funerals—he tried, but it was embarrassing.

What do you do with sensitive men? More significant perhaps, what does God do with them? I know what he does with some—he turns them into preachers; and of all the preachers the world has ever heard, sitting on the edges of the pews, Jeremiah, the hyper-sensitive, was undoubtedly the father.

You can't do anything with people unless you are sensitive. Pity the patient who finds himself in hospital tended by a nurse who isn't sensitive. Pity the school that has for Headmaster a man whose nature is thick and wooden. Pity the audience listening to a pianist skilled in technique but lacking all soul. Sensitiveness is the key to all great artistry, sensitiveness of soul.

But some people are thick. And it was the destiny of Jeremiah to be called to preach at a time when most people were thick. Their passions burst from them like fat boys bursting their seams. They sniffed like dogs, and neighed like horses, quivering to gratify their lusts. And the women turned harlot lay sprawling in every dark corner. And amidst all this sweating heap of brutish humanity God called hyper-sensitive Jeremiah to witness to himself.

A little while ago, in a historical novel of seventeenth-century life in Paris, I read of a priest called for the first time in his life to act as chaplain to a marquise condemned to beheading in the Place de Greve. How could he do it? How could he kneel there, holding her hand before that vulgar staring mob, reciting in Latin the "Salve" as the sword fell by the headsman's hand. But he did it. There is courage of a kind not always counted. It is courage of the sensitive who do not shrink from facing lewdness.

And such was Jeremiah. Indeed I do not think in all the scriptures there is a man to be compared to him for such quality of courage—unless it be our Lord himself walking to his crucifixion. But this is the measure of Jeremiah's greatness, that he never abandoned the people he served. They guffawed at him; they belched at him; they imprisoned him; they tried to drown him in a pit in which was only slime to suck him under; but still he never ran away.

Preachers aren't made in any preaching school. They are sensitive souls whose will is to shrink from all the mean and tawdry, but this they never do. They never do it because they know how easily they could sink to such a level, and might indeed be there were it not for the Grace of God so freely given.

But they understand people. There never was a preacher whom congregations hoped might preach again who did not understand people. Such was Jeremiah's secret. He understood the human heart. Were you a shy man, a silly man, a stupid man, a solemn man, Jeremiah knew all about you and told you just as much in words or more till you ask in consternation, as Nathaniel asked of Jesus, "Whence knowest thou me?" Shakespeare was like that, and Dostoevsky, and all the creative artists of the world's great literature. They give you entrance to a murderer's heart, a coward's heart, a glutton's heart, a hero's heart, a faithful mother's heart, till you cry aloud in wonder, How can he know all this? Could he perchance have been a murderer, coward, glutton, hero, mother, father, child, and son? How *does* he know, how *can* he know what it feels to be such characters as these? And the answer is—through sensitivity.

Extreme sensitiveness is a burden to be borne. In many ways it makes life harder. It sharpens pain, it deepens depression, it wearies the body, it wearies the nerves. Sensitive people are shy, they retire from the crowd; fears loom up, even unfounded fears, and all this makes the body thin. For the comfortable life—better be a gourmand, better be coarse; but know this, that all the creative work in reading people stems from sensitiveness which is costly in strength.

And there you have the key to Jeremiah, the key to his shyness—"Oh Lord God I am but a child I cannot speak"; the key to his anguish—"I am become a laughing stock all the day, everyone mocketh me"; the key to his Jeremiad because this was the man who was called to minister at a time when Israel's morals sank in decaying putrefaction. No wonder he shrank from it, no wonder he cried over it. But he never left these people, nor ever ran away. Such was the courage of Jeremiah, and such was his greatness.

And because he was such an expert in reading the human heart, it was in the heart that he sought all true religion. There was a majority opinion in his day that a man could only be in touch with God if he stood on Israel's soil. There was also a majority opinion that a man could only be in touch with God in the presence of the appropriate ceremony. And there came a king, by name Josiah, who put his trust in ecclesiastical reform. And, mark you, there is truth in all these views. We need to be in touch with sacred places, we must have ceremony in our public worship, and how great the scandal if the Church's house is grossly out of order. But this is the great truth Jeremiah shouted from the housetops, none of these is the heart of religion, neither conformity nor nonconformity, neither Low Church nor High Church, neither tidy ecclesiastical organisation nor untidy ecclesiastical organisation. None of these things saves a man from himself, they do not give courage to the coward, nor confidence to the sinner. Only when the heart of man is reached, only when the heart of man is touched by the word of the living God, touched by fire, touched by love, burnt and refined and remade, only then is religion in its stride; and because Jeremiah could minister this, a religion of the heart which touched the heart, Jeremiah has remained the father of all the worlds' great preachers whom congregations wish to hear again.

Listen to him:

Behold, the days come, saith the Lord, that I will make a new covenant with the House of Israel, and with the House of Judah: not according to the covenant that I made with their fathers in the day that I took them by the hand to bring them out of the land of Egypt: which my covenant they brake . . . but this is the covenant . . . I will put my law in their inward parts, and in their heart will I write it . . . and they shall teach no more every man his neighbour . . . saying, Know the Lord: for they shall all know me, from the least of them unto the greatest . . . for I will forgive their iniquity, and their sin will I remember no more.

And of whom does all this remind you? Is it not of Christ himself in the days of his flesh? Reading people, spurned by people, mixing with people, staying with people, rebuking them, forgiving them, loving them, giving them each in his heart what each man needed. Sensitive, yes; a man of sorrows, yes; Jeremiah, yes; but this was the means by which he read the depths of every human heart, and came to meet them at their point of greatest human need.

This is the true preacher. Not a man with the gift of the gab. Not a man with a First in theology, nor any kind of ecclesiastical diplomat. He might be these, but first he is a sensitive man who has himself found God in the secret place of his own soul, meeting his own need, speaking to his own condition. That is the man who speaks to others, that is the man through whom God speaks. And this is what he says. . . .

There is no situation in which a man finds himself where God cannot come to meet his need. God can meet him in Babylon as Jeremiah said, or in Piccadilly Circus or the Gloucester Road; in depression or in elation; in fear, in repose; in hot sunshine or in the darkness; in church, in the theatre; in company, alone; because the place where God is only really met is the secret place of a man's own soul, and that he takes about with him wherever he may go. That is the comfort of the gospel, there is no place a man can be where God with his succour cannot also be. But we must let him in, *we* have the key. And no small part of my task, no small part of every preacher's task, is to bid you turn that key. Then God comes in, comes in to your situation. And then the room is changed—the old furniture is there, the old problems are there, but they look different. And when you accept them in his presence you find you can go on. God's strength is made perfect in our weakness. That is what the prophet found alone inside his heart, and so can everyone of us. . . . And that is real religion.

6. THE CALL OF GOD'S SERVANT

AMOS, CHAPTER 7, VV. 10-17

*Then Amaziah the priest of Beth-el sent to Jeroboam King
of Israel, saying, Amos hath conspired against thee in the midst
of the house of Israel: the land is not able to bear all his words.
For thus Amos saith, Jeroboam shall die by the sword, and Israel
shall surely be led away captive out of his land. Also Amaziah
said unto Amos, O thou seer, go, flee thee away into the land of
Judah, and there eat bread, and prophesy there: but prophesy not
again any more at Beth-el: for it is the King's sanctuary, and it
is a royal house.*

*Then answered Amos, and said to Amaziah, I was no prophet,
neither was I a prophet's son; but I was an herdman, and a
dresser of sycomore trees; and the Lord took me from following
the flock, and the Lord said unto me, Go, prophesy unto my
people Israel. Now therefore hear thou the word of the Lord:
Thou sayest, Prophesy not against Israel, and drop not thy
word against the house of Isaac; therefore thus saith the Lord:
Thy wife shall be an harlot in the city, and thy sons and thy
daughters shall fall by the sword, and thy land shall be divided
by line; and thou thyself shalt die in a land that is unclean, and
Israel shall surely be led away captive out of his land.*

AMOS 7, vv. 14, 15: I was no prophet, neither
was I a prophet's son; but I was an herdman, and
a dresser of sycomore trees; and the Lord took
me from following the flock, and the Lord said
unto me, Go, prophesy unto my people Israel.

"I was no prophet, neither was I a prophet's son"—you can
prove that for yourself if you have the patience; you can

175

search all through the scriptures till you are tired of searching, and you will not find anywhere the name of the father of Amos, nor the name of any religious organisation in which he was reared; and yet it was through this man that God shook Israel, and, in time to come, many nations in far distant times in the matter of social justice.

"I was no prophet, neither was I a prophet's son." Amos never grew accustomed to the strangeness of the fact that he of all people should have been called of God to be his servant and mouthpiece to a wayward people. For he was a mouthpiece. He was like John the Baptist in the wilderness, a voice, a voice with no distinguished antecedents, no one in fact worth giving a label to at all.

"I was no prophet, neither was I a prophet's son" . . . I used to look after cows. I did that in the spring and winter when the rains made sufficient pasture upon the hills of Judah; and in the summer when the hills were parched and burnt I trekked down to the coastal plain there to spend my time dressing sycomore trees before the fruit came on; strange that *I* should be called to be God's mouthpiece.

But is it strange? Is it strange in the annals of God's Church? Listen to St. Paul addressing the Corinthians: "Not many wise after the flesh, not many mighty, not many noble . . . but God chose the foolish things of the world . . . and the weak things . . . and the base things . . and the things that were despised . . ." (I Corinthians 1, vv. 26-28). "I was no prophet, neither was I a prophet's son"—I used to look after cows, but the Lord took me.

When you leave this Cathedral[1] this morning, ask, if you dare, the first six people you meet what the love of God means to them. You can guess the result! But this is what I should like to ask you if I may, Why does it mean something to you? How do you explain it? Why are *you* a communicant? How is it that *you* are a praying man, and a worshipping man, and a believing man? Why aren't you a scoffer? or a cynic? or one

---

[1] Bradford Cathedral.

of those many thousands completely unmoved by any kind of religion? This is what I would like to say to everyone individually this morning—if you are not in tune with all this strangeness of the call of God to you, that you (of all people) should be privileged to know God's peace in your heart, then, my friend, you have no part nor lot with those who throughout the ages have been called the servants of the most high God.

For God's calling *is* strange. St. Paul was a persecutor. Augustine was licentious. Luther was born at the back of an open stall in the market of Eisleben and could not say the words "Our Father" without a shudder because they reminded him of his own coarse father. Carey was a cobbler. Kagawa, the son of a Geisha girl. Strange that God should choose these men to shake whole countries with his words . . . but is it more strange that he has chosen you to be his witness in the circumstances in which you labour five days in each week. Why have not your associates sufficient faith to make them worship? Why have you? Amos never grew accustomed to the strangeness of his call: "I was no prophet, neither was I a prophet's son." I used to look after cows. We haven't grasped the nature of our faith till we have pondered the fact that we did not choose it all ourselves, but God chose us, and why he did, we may never know. . . .

And someone wishes to object. What you say is suitable for Amos, St. Paul, St. Augustine, Luther, Carey; these were the great men, you can stress the strangeness of their call. But we are the ordinary worshippers, the laity, the rank and file. Are you? But all Christians in the New Testament are called "elect" or "chosen". Do you call yourself a Christian? Then you are elect, elect of God. I know you may not be a prophet, but a housewife, a company director, a retired civil servant, a secretary; but God has chosen you. Why? I cannot tell. But no one is brought to the faith for his own comfort, no one is saved for his own salvation, but that he may also be a helping hand to other people near him.

*   *   *

And now we dig a little. "I was no prophet, neither was I a prophet's son; but I was an herdman and dresser of sycomore trees." Was it after all so strange that God should choose a man like this? Amos was a rugged man. Amos was an open-air man, a man accustomed to deal with nature in the raw. And such were the qualities necessary at a time when the men of Israel were falsely inflated with the fictitious wealth of Jeroboam's reign. They needed plain speaking, they even needed bluntness, and this is what they heard from Amos, herdman of Tekoa and dresser of sycomore trees.

And when we dig a little deeper into the life of St. Paul the persecutor we can see some of the reasonableness of choosing this unworthy man if God's purpose was to show that human salvation does not depend on human worthiness—but on the grace of God. And we can see why Augustine was chosen, Augustine the rhetoric professor of Rome, if God's purpose was to clothe the gospel in words for Europe for a period of well-nigh one thousand years. And was there not reason why Luther was chosen, a man of powerful instincts at a time when instincts were running riot in the lives of men.

> God moves in a mysterious way
> His wonders to perform;

but it is not for nothing that

> He plants His footsteps in the sea,
> And rides upon the storm.

And our minds run on to Jesus. Did he learn those parables? Did he learn that parabolic, that story-telling method in the public ministry in Galilee? I do not think so. There were younger children in the Nazareth home, and after Joseph died Jesus learnt the art of holding their attention while his mother Mary did the housework . . . at least, I shouldn't wonder.

The point is, God uses backgrounds. I was going to say, God arranges backgrounds, and I am not so sure it isn't true —God certainly chooses his servants with respect to backgrounds. The longer I labour in the Christian ministry, the more I see how limited is my ministry just because I am a professional and make my living by this means. But you don't. You're a housewife, a company director, a clerk or a secretary. No one can say you're paid to be good. No one can say it's worth your while to be a Christian. And so, because of your background, God has chosen you to be his servant. In your own person you carry the Christian way of life into the secular callings where people earn their daily bread. Never say, "How can I be God's servant, I am a booking clerk." You were chosen because you *are* a booking clerk. God wants his witness in the place where booking clerks labour.

* * *

And one more point. "I was no prophet, neither was I a prophet's son . . . but the Lord took me . . . and . . . said unto me, Go, prophesy unto my people Israel."

Amos said that in the royal sanctuary at Bethel when the priest in charge accosted him for unauthorised preaching— "O thou seer, go, flee thee away into the land of Judah, and there eat bread, and prophesy there."

Was Amos afraid to be thus rebuked by the royal officer? If he was he steadied himself by the thought of his call. . . . He hadn't chosen to be a prophet as men might choose some other profession. He was a herdman and dresser of sycomore trees, but the *Lord* said unto him, "Go, prophesy to my people Israel."

I am not speaking to you from books now. Books I value and to books I am indebted; but when a man has set himself to wrestle for the souls of men, it is not books he needs, but experience drawn from life. And the only way I can find confidence to do those things allotted to my care, involving as it does speaking in the name of God, sometimes to individuals, sometimes to tens of thousands at a time, the only way I can find confidence as to why people should take it from my lips is that years ago now when I had thought to pursue a scientific career, I heard in my teens a voice saying to me: "Go, take up the Christian ministry. . . ." "I was no prophet, neither was I a prophet's son . . . but the Lord took me and said, Go, prophesy to my people Israel."

My friend, have you no such time when "the things of God" first began to make your heart beat faster? No time when, from being a formal routine thing of duty the Christian faith spoke plainly of the other world? I'm not so inexperienced as to imagine that life is like that every day, but if there is some moment, or period of time, in your life when God was real to you, treasure it; some day when you're afraid, you'll need it, and it will give you greater confidence. Remember religion, real religion, is never grounded in some fancy whim which once you had; it is grounded in God reaching down to touch your life. "I was no prophet, neither was I a prophet's son . . . but the Lord took me . . ." or, as Jesus said to his disciples, "Ye have not chosen me but I have chosen you. . . ."

7. A WINDOW ON GOD

HOSEA, CHAPTER 11, VV. 1-9

When Israel was a child, then I loved him, and called my son out of Egypt. As they called them, so they went from them: they sacrificed unto the Baalim, and burned incense to graven images. Yet I taught Ephraim to go; I took them on my arms; but they knew not that I healed them. I drew them with cords of a man, with bands of love; and I was to them as they that take off the yoke on their jaws, and I laid meat before them. He shall not return into the land of Egypt; but the Assyrian shall be his king, because they refused to return. And the sword shall fall upon his cities, and shall consume his bars, and devour them, because of their own counsels. And my people are bent to backsliding from me: though they call them to him that is on high, none at all will exalt him.

How shall I give thee up, Ephraim? How shall I deliver thee, Israel? How shall I make thee as Admah? How shall I set thee as Zeboim? Mine heart is turned within me, my compassions are kindled together. I will not execute the fierceness of mine anger, I will not return to destroy Ephraim: for I am God and not man; the Holy One in the midst of thee: and I will not enter into the city.

HOSEA 11, v. 8: How shall I give thee up, Ephraim? How shall I deliver thee, Israel?

A SHORT time ago I met a man carrying a bunch of flowers. I had seen him before in the street, but I had never spoken to him; but this time I did. I mentioned the flowers. He smiled, looked down at the bunch, turning it this way and that, and commented, "Funny thing, had to buy them—looked rather pretty. Can't arrange them though. Shall stick them in a jug.

You see, I live alone. . . . Now my wife, she was good at it, *wonderful* what she could do with flowers. Ah, well . . ." And he passed on down the street, carrying his flowers, upside down, as men do, rather self-consciously.

Late that night when I saw a light in his flat, I thought of him sitting there alone with his flowers in a jug. I wanted to call, but I didn't dare. . . . And then I thought of all the lonely people in London, some bereaved, some exiled, some ever friendless, but, most pitiful of all perhaps, the deserted (my heart goes out to them), deserted by wife or deserted by husband, and now they are alone when they needn't be alone. That is the bitterness of *their* case.

And such a one was Hosea in the Old Testament, sitting alone in his empty house. And it's all so long ago, but human hearts were much the same in 745 B.C. as they are in A.D. 1960, and loneliness hasn't changed its taste.

Loneliness is connected with longing, and longing is connected with love. And love is a strange emotion, so real but so intangible, a spiritual force even the materialistically minded have to reckon with. Some, of course, dismiss it as sex, but that is merely biological; others connect it only with the family, but that is sociological. But the truth is, love is metaphysical. It deals with that which lies beyond the range of human reckoning. And so we need not be surprised that love or even loneliness should be a window opening on to God.

And this is what Hosea found. And this is why we have his story in our Bibles. Not merely that he married a woman and she left him. Not merely that he sat there brooding with a broken heart. You can find that, alas, in Kensington. Not even that Hosea went with money to buy her back from a common brothel. That is most unusual. But Hosea's story is in our Bibles because his love, his longing, his loneliness became for him a window opening on to God.

Do you find this comforting? I hope you do. There is nothing that can come to us, however heart-disrupting, that cannot be in the last resort a window on to God. The blunt, surprising, no, even startling, truth is that in the Bible the nature of God was *first* most deeply perceived by a man sitting alone in the ruins of his broken home, his wife gone, the children left there, not his own, at least he wasn't sure.

Oh, thank heaven, few are called to see God through this darkened window. There are many other windows which by far most men come to use. But Hosea used it, used it to see into the heart of God, seeing, through the longing that he felt to have this woman back, how God feels. "How shall I give thee up, Ephraim? How shall I deliver thee, Israel?" He saw that, however true it is that men have left God far behind in all their worldly thoughts, God never casts us off, forgets, or lets his heart be hardened. As Hosea wanted his prodigal wife back, as the father in the New Testament wanted his prodigal son back, so the eternal God aches to have his children back: "How shall I give thee up, Ephraim? How shall I deliver thee, Israel?"

* * *

I would hazard a guess that you think of God firstly as a lawmaker. You are not wrong. It was the service of Israel's first great writing prophet, Amos, that he showed how moral laws lie deep embedded in our life; and if men break them, break them for their private gain, breaking of their world will be their bitter ending—"The lion has roared who will not fear . . ." It is a warning for all the brothel-running, drug-selling, and money-fiddling going on in London now. But this is what Hosea saw, not a judge enraged by broken laws, but a lover alone with his head in his hands, broken by desertion. And that is God: it is a revelation.

And someone is thinking, I suppose, then it doesn't matter how flagrantly we sin, there is no retribution. God is more hurt than affronted. And it certainly is true—God never strikes a single soul because he has forsworn him. Hosea never took his wife aside and beat her for a punishment. He cried over her, and ached over her, and tried to woo her still; but when she dragged her spiritless limbs out from the brothel, he saw in her eyes that were as dead as stone that she had punishment enough.

183

This is the lesson. Spurned love brings its own punishment. There is no need to add more on. When love is pure and right and sacrificial of itself (which is what love is embedded in the heart of God) and *we* laugh at it, scorn it, trample on it and desert it, we are not the same again. True, we still have eyes and hair and face and limbs, but the spirit at the back of all goes dead and life responds to no more kindling.

That is what Hosea saw when the girl he loved came home again. God's love will never die, that is what he saw (even though men crucify it); but if men trample on it long, without repenting, they will drag about within their bodies a shattered human spirit with consequences sore in political life as well as in domestic.

This is what Hosea tells us in his book. It is a book of beauty, but a book of shattered beauty. It is as if a man has taken a stone to cast with all his strength at our beautiful east window. And there follows an ear-splitting crash and a splintering of glass, and all the lovely pieces lie scattered on this marble floor, beautiful in themselves as pieces, but making nothing of a pattern. So is Hosea's book, sentences here, sentences there, gleaming sentences—"Israel is a cake not turned"; "Ephraim is like a silly dove"; "Gray hairs are here and there upon him, and he knoweth it not". But try to analyse the book and you will find the pattern difficult to trace.

And then you come to the last chapter. I sometimes wonder if there is anything more beautiful in all the Old Testament than the fourteenth chapter of Hosea. You have read of desertion. You have read of love; a new word "chesed", meaning loving kindness the author introduces, and you have looked at the gaunt results of spiritual decay. But then, at last, a freshness breaks upon the barren scene, a lovely picture of repentance making for renewal as in a watered garden—"Take with you words and return unto the Lord: say unto him, Take away all iniquity and accept that which is good: so will we render as bullocks the offering of our lips. Asshur shall not save us: we will not ride upon horses: neither will we say any more to the work of our hands, Ye

184

are our gods: for in thee the fatherless findeth mercy ('chesed'). I will heal their backsliding, I will love them freely: for mine anger is turned away from him. I will be as the dew unto Israel: he shall blossom as the lily, and cast forth his roots as Lebanon."

* * *

Am I addressing someone this evening who has tasted bitterness in his life? My friend, I wish with all my heart that this had never come your way. But if it has, it *could* turn out to be perhaps in the end a window on to God. That is what Hosea learnt.

And this is what he also says. Don't think of God as a vindictive judge. God is never that. God cares and God loves, though if we go on spurning love we shatter in the end the beauty that we have and that is retribution.

And thirdly, this: We can come back. Everyone can come back. And if we do, new life begins again because God is ever waiting still to give it. That is the gospel of the Old Testament. That is the gospel in the New Testament. God is a God of loving kindness ("chesed"), and we only hurt ourselves when we refuse to have it so.

Love divine, all loves excelling,
Joy of Heav'n, to earth come down;
Fix in us thy humble dwelling,
All thy faithful mercies crown.

(C. Wesley, 1747.)

8. THE PRINCIPLE OF ACCEPTANCE

HAGGAI, CHAPTER 1, VV. 3-11; CHAPTER 2, V. 4

*Then came the word of the Lord by Haggai the prophet,
saying, Is it a time for you yourselves to dwell in your cieled
houses, while this house lieth waste? Now therefore thus saith
the Lord of hosts: Consider your ways. Ye have sown much, and
bring in little; ye eat, but ye have not enough; ye drink, but ye
are not filled with drink; ye clothe you, but there is none warm;
and he that earneth wages earneth wages to put it into a bag
with holes. Thus saith the Lord of hosts: Consider your ways.
Go up to the mountain, and bring wood, and build the house;
and I will take pleasure in it, and I will be glorified, saith the
Lord. Ye looked for much, and, lo, it came to little; and when
ye brought it home, I did blow upon it. Why? saith the Lord of
hosts. Because of mine house that lieth waste, while ye run every
man to his own house. Therefore for your sake the heaven is
stayed from dew, and the earth is stayed from her fruit. And I
called for a drought upon the land, and upon the mountains, and
upon the corn, and upon the wine, and upon the oil, and upon
that which the ground bringeth forth, and upon men, and upon
cattle, and upon all the labour of the hands.*

*Yet now be strong, O Zerubbabel, saith the Lord; and be
strong, O Joshua, son of Jehozadak, the high priest; and be
strong, all ye people of the land, saith the Lord, and work:
for I am with you, saith the Lord of hosts.*

HAGGAI 2, v. 4: . . . Be strong . . . and work:
for I am with you, saith the Lord of hosts.

ON Monday of last week, I met a man in Regent Street,
listless, lifeless, and disgruntled. I could scarcely believe my

eyes because I knew him once as full of wit and energy. But he had changed his job, and he was wringing his hands. He said he'd made his life's mistake, no other chance would come his way, there was little left for him to do. I was sorry, I was also embarrassed; truth to tell, I didn't know exactly what to say standing there in Regent Street; and I can't be certain that this man was even pleased to see me. So I left him, thinking as I made my way along the crowded street—nothing will come to this man unless he learns the principle of acceptance. . . .

I shouldn't wonder if you aren't a little tired of hearing me stress this doctrine of acceptance, the acceptance of what comes to us in life. You complain—how can a man develop himself? How can a Christian be anything else but a common lazybones, or our environment ever be bettered if the proper way of living is acceptance of the status quo. Look what cruelties, injustices, slums, and downright stupidities would have lasted had your doctrine of acceptance been the way for all. Surely anybody in his senses must see that a man's got to bestir himself, fulfil himself, exert himself—"make hay while the sun shines"—if ever he will hope to prosper. After all, it's the weakest that go to the wall. . . . Such, I fancy, are some of the objections I can overhear raised against the doctrine of acceptance.

For I *do* teach it. I make no bones about it. I *do* teach it, here in Prince Consort Road. Time and time again I teach from this pulpit that there is no peace of mind available, no hidden resource of strength obtainable, and therefore, no poise, resistance, nor courage that can laugh in the face of adversity, unless and until a man has learnt how to accept what comes to him in life, some of it exceedingly puzzling, as somehow within the good purposes of God.

I wouldn't like you to think that this is a private doctrine of mine. It is taught wherever Christianity is taught. And not only Christianity, that is the remarkable fact. It is almost the essence of Taoism and occupies a place within the practice of the Hindu and the Buddhist. The way of peace in life is the way of acceptance. . . .

And now you hear my text to-day—". . . Be strong . . . and work: for I am with you, saith the Lord of hosts." And you breathe a sigh of relief. At last, here's a man's religion: "Heaven helps those who help themselves"; "God is on the side of the big battalions." And you warm to Haggai. You don't know much about Haggai in the Old Testament, but you warm to him. "Be strong and work, for I am with you, saith the Lord of hosts." He's a man after your own common-sense religion.

But are you sure you're right? Does enterprise come before acceptance, and not acceptance before enterprise? Are you sure you're right?

Look at Haggai. Look at his history, his mission, and his book. Never was a people so dispirited as in his day, the second year of Darius the King. They'd tried, God knows they'd tried. They had in their land a housing programme, an agriculture programme, and a money programme; but nothing ever seemed to prosper. Listen!

"Ye have sown much and bring in little; ye eat but you have not enough; ye drink but ye are not filled with drink; ye clothe you, but there is none warm; and he that earneth wages earneth wages to put it into a bag with holes." (Haggai 1, v. 6). Have you no imagination? Can't you see them? Drab faces! Drab clothes! Dead eyes! They are the picture of some listless soul crying bitterly from out the depths of bitter disappointment—"I'm just not getting anywhere at all."

You must remember it was seventeen years since the Jewish exiles came back from Babylon with a song on their lips and a light in their eyes. Seventeen years since they were like youths bracing themselves for the battle of life. They'd rolled up their sleeves, they'd sharpened their tools. But the rains held off and the crops were thin. What was worse, even God seemed bent to blast their noble enterprise—"Ye looked for much, and lo, it came to little; and when ye brought it home, I did blow upon it" (Haggai 1, v. 9).

So what do you do? What *can* you do when people are disheartened? What can you do to lift them up to work and
188

life and laughter? Tell them to work and live and laugh? Not if you have any heart you don't; not if you have any brains you don't. How will they do the very thing they cannot do? If all you have to say is: "Pull yourself together," they will answer blankly with the truth "Why? Why should I? What difference will it make?"

Surely here is the blunt truth about us human beings. We wilt if we feel we are forsaken. See the woman unloved, see the man unloved. They wilt, they lose heart in their clothes, they lose heart in their work. The truth is, we bestir ourselves when we feel it worth the effort. We rise to live when someone cares for us.

And so the first call from this pulpit is never—"Do this, do that, do the other." Nor is it from any other Christian pulpit in so far as it understands the basic Christian message. The first utterance is a statement: God is a Father who loves you, so loves you that he sent his Son to die for you, and you matter to him always.

Hear then Haggai as he should be heard. Hear him as those people in Judea heard him five hundred and twenty years before Messiah came, hearing as they stood with horny, blistered, work-worn hands propped up by their tools. It was not the call to work which made them try again; it was the reassurance of the fact that God was with them still. "Be strong and work, for I am with you, saith the Lord of hosts."

And still you do not understand. You show me your setbacks, you describe your loneliness, you tell of frustrations making life so very empty. And I do not rationalise these things all away. Remember, I, too, the preacher, know half-empty barns. But this is what I teach—the doctrine of acceptance, the faith that even these frustrating facts come somehow in the providence of God. "I am with you," saith the Lord of hosts. Yes, in spite of those setbacks, even co-operating with those setbacks, for my purposes of good. I love you. I care for you. I will never lose you. This is the message of the scriptures. This is the constant word of God. And who has ears to hear it in the presence of his setbacks rises up to live his life again. You can see it by his clothes.

And still you want some further confirmation. So look at your history book. Look at the Calvinists, Presbyterian Calvinists if you like, Scottish Presbyterian Calvinists if you know them well. Are they lazy people? Are they unenterprising people? What kind of people were largely responsible for the settling of the North Americas? You see, acceptance of a plan of God for human life on earth does not result in laissez faire. It results in the reverse. If God loves me, I shall not wilt, but rise to meet him on the way. And I am no Calvinist, for all the respect I have for Calvin of Geneva; but I believe in a providence of God which makes for human enterprise.

So I come back to Haggai. "Go up to the mountains," he said to those dispirited peoples. "Bring wood and build the house and I will take pleasure in it." Reconstruct in your midst the sign of my presence in your midst. Then you will have life, then you will have energy, then you will prosper. And they did go up to the mountains and they did bring wood, and they did build the house and they did prosper. Not all at once, but in due time. It is the only way. First faith, then acceptance, then enterprise. So do not turn this doctrine down, the doctrine of acceptance; it makes for peace, it makes for enterprise. "Be strong and work, *for I am with you*, saith the Lord of hosts," or in the words of St. Paul, "Work out your own salvation with fear and trembling; for it is God which worketh in you both to will and to work for his good pleasure" (Philippians 2, v. 12).

9. WHEN PREACHING IS EFFECTIVE

And Paul stood up, and beckoning with the hand said, Men of Israel, and ye that fear God, hearken. The God of this people Israel chose our fathers, and exalted the people when they sojourned in the land of Egypt, and with a high arm led he them forth out of it. And for about the time of forty years suffered he their manners in the wilderness.

And when he had destroyed seven nations in the land of Canaan, he gave them their land for an inheritance, for about four hundred and fifty years: and after these things he gave them judges until Samuel the prophet. And afterward they asked for a King: and God gave unto them Saul the son of Kish, a man of the tribe of Benjamin, for the space of forty years. And when he had removed him, he raised up David to be their King; to whom also he bare witness, and said, I have found David the son of Jesse, a man after my heart, who shall do all my will. Of this man's seed hath God according to promise brought unto Israel a Saviour, Jesus; when John had first preached before his coming the baptism of repentance to all the people of Israel. And as John was fulfilling his course, he said, What suppose ye that I am? I am not he. But behold, there cometh one after me, the shoes of whose feet I am not worthy to unloose.

Brethren, children of the stock of Abraham, and those among you that fear God, to us is the word of this salvation sent forth. For they that dwell in Jerusalem, and their rulers, because they knew him not, nor the voices of the prophets which are read every sabbath, fulfilled them by condemning him. And though they found no cause of death in him, yet asked they of Pilate that he should be slain. And when they had fulfilled all things that were written of him, they took him down from the tree, and laid him in a tomb. But God raised him from the dead: and

he was seen for many days of them that came up with him from
Galilee to Jerusalem, who are now his witnesses unto the people.

And we bring you good tidings of the promise made unto the
fathers, how that God hath fulfilled the same unto our children,
in that he raised up Jesus; as also it is written in the second
psalm, Thou art my Son, this day have I begotten thee. And as
concerning that he raised him up from the dead, now no more to
return to corruption, he hath spoken on this wise, I will give you
the holy and sure blessings of David. Because he saith also in
another psalm, Thou wilt not give thy Holy One to see corruption.
For David, after he had in his own generation served the counsel
of God, fell on sleep, and was laid unto his fathers, and saw
corruption: but he whom God raised up saw no corruption.

Be it known unto you therefore, brethren, that through this
man is proclaimed unto you remission of sins: and by him every
one that believeth is justified from all things, from which ye
could not be justified by the law of Moses.

Beware, therefore, lest that come upon you, which is spoken in
the prophets:

> *Behold, ye despisers, and wonder, and perish;*
> *For I work a work in your days,*
> *A work which ye shall in no wise believe,*
> *If one declare it unto you.*

And as they went out, they besought that these words might
be spoken to them the next sabbath.

Now when the synagogue broke up, many of the Jews and of
the devout proselytes followed Paul and Barnabas: who,
speaking to them, urged them to continue in the grace of God.

~~~~~~

ACTS 13, v. 42: And as they went out, they
besought that these words might be spoken to
them the next sabbath.

~~~~~~

I WONDER if you have thought to yourself "I'd like to hear
that sermon again". I wonder if you've even thought "I'd

192

like to get hold of that sermon for myself and read it through on my own". Perhaps you can't imagine yourself ever being in such a position with regard to any sermon. The very word to you smacks of dullness, dryness, and boredom—a sermon! Oh dear, a sermon!

That was how most people felt about sermons in the old synagogues in the first century of our era; but one day there came a different kind of preacher—and after they had heard him "as they went out they besought that these words might be spoken to them the next Sabbath."

I wonder why they did that. I've asked myself that question: and since we possess a copy of that sermon (It constituted the second lesson to this morning's service), I've examined it to try to ascertain why it produced this result. And these are my conclusions.

First, it interpreted history. No, it wasn't a history lesson, let there be no misunderstanding, it wasn't history in general, it was *their* history, their own national and their own personal history. Paul in this sermon in Antioch in Pisidia showed them what God was doing in their lives.

A few days ago I had lunch with a man with whom I wanted to keep in touch. He was an Australian with a good war record in the Malayan jungle, but when I first met him he was unbaptized, unconfirmed, certainly no professing believer. Now he is a churchwarden. We talked about Church. We also talked about *his* profession. But by the time we had reached the sweet course at lunch we were talking about personal gifts, the call of God and divine providence. How boring! you say. How dull! Much better to talk about politics. Was it? I don't think I am overstating the case when I say that my friend went away with new confidence for his work as a professional man here in London. All because what we had talked about was an interpretation of personal experience, his and mine and other people's. . . .

And sermons can do that, and when they do, they live. That frustration a year or two ago which still rankles, how do I face it? That turn for the better in my fortunes when least I expected it, what confidence it has given! That complicated personal relationship at the moment, what ought I to do about it? Sermons live when they help us here. . . . "And as they went out they besought that these words might be spoken to them the next Sabbath."

*　　*　　*

And then examining the sermon once more, I note that it interpreted the scriptures. The days are not yet gone as they ought to be when preachers concoct sermons of their own and then hang them on texts as if they were nails for pictures on the walls. This ought not to be. The Bible is the Church's treasure; buried treasure perhaps, buried for most people, buried for some clergy. But it is their task to dig it up and show it. And when they do, it never fails to draw.

But this implies work, spade work, digging work. "How long did it take you to prepare that sermon?" someone asked a preacher once, and this was the reply: "Fifty years or thereabouts."

I wonder how long we must wait before this exposition of the scriptures returns again to Anglican pulpits. But instead we get addresses or talks or meditations. Anything but a sermon, because a sermon is the product of laborious digging, and this too few engage in.

*　　*　　*

Thirdly, I notice this sermon preached by Paul in Antioch appealed to human need.

I remember years ago, when I was a student, straying from my own religious denomination (as students do so very understandably) and visiting the City Temple. I was working hard then, perhaps overworking, but I wanted to win a good degree. And I grew frightened. I suppose I was overtired. But I thought, "Suppose I fall ill the night before the examination, suppose I see the questions on the examination paper and my mind is in a whirl and I write rubbish!" I thought of those who had put confidence in me. I thought of that strange tarred summer-house I told you of where I received my earliest inspiration. And then I went to the City Temple. It was a layman preaching, a lecturer in Ancient History in the University of Cambridge. I sat rooted to the pew. It was a sermon on God's strengthening power in time of temptation. I can see him now. An ugly man in an ugly church, but the grace of God was on his lips. He preached to my need. I gained the stiffening he so eloquently talked about. And you won't be hard on me if I tell you that I, an Anglican, returned there the next Sunday to worship with the Congregationalists, to hear those words again. "And as they went out they besought that these words might be spoken to them the next Sabbath."

* * *

I wonder what are our human needs to-day? Much the same I suppose as they ever were. Courage for the morrow. Confidence that what has happened to me (some of it strange) is somehow in the plan of God. Forgiveness, God's forgiveness, for the stupid things I've done throughout the years. And I can only give my testimony—if a preacher gives those things to me, I'll go and hear him next Sunday, and the Sunday after just like these people in Antioch who "as they went out besought that these words might be spoken to them the next Sabbath."

When I was first ordained, it wasn't to a ministry in a church but to a lectureship, and so I had my Sundays free. And time and time again I used to worship in a famous church where the music was superb. But something distressed me. It was the number of people who slipped out in the hymn before the sermon. Not one not two, but thirty, forty, fifty. And not because of children (which is understandable). But perhaps for them God slipped out before the sermon. I do not know. It might be the preacher's fault. It might be the people's fault. But man in pulpit *and* people in pew might cause God to slip out in the hymn before the sermon. . . .

And this surprises you. I mean, it surprises you that the congregation has anything to do with the sermon—except perhaps to try to stop yawning. But it has. A congregation creates the preacher it deserves. I know this. A preacher can preach a sermon in one church with uplifting power, and he can preach the same sermon in another church and simply nothing happens. I know it. Dame Edith Evans said something very like this about her art too. And the late Kathleen Ferrier.

I am sure the first responsibility rests upon the preacher. He is the leader, he is the minister; but when that is said a hundred times we must start saying something about the responsibility of the congregation. Does it want to hear? That is a governing factor. I am absolutely certain Paul preached a good sermon in Antioch in Pisidia the next sabbath because "as they went out the people besought that these words might be spoken to them the next Sabbath." They wanted to hear.

And Christian worshippers should pray for the preacher. Perhaps they think he doesn't *need* praying for, or is *past* praying for; but unless they pray, nothing very much will happen: in fact, God may slip out just before the sermon.

And then this: A congregation should own their preacher. What I mean is this. They should in some degree count his words as an expression of *their* faith: as our hymns and psalms and prayers uttered in this place are our act of corporate worship, so the sermon is our corporate expression in Kensington of what we ourselves partly believe. The preacher belongs to the congregation. They should own him.

And so it is that a congregation creates the preacher it deserves. Does it want to hear its preacher? Does it ever pray for its preacher? Does it count the words he says as in some part their faith? Then that church will grow. It will become strong. It will be effective. First the ministry does depend on the minister. But it also depends on the congregation. And when the two are faithful, God's presence there is felt . . . and people are uplifted.

Let us pray:

> Within these walls let holy peace,
> And love, and concord dwell;
> Here give the troubled conscience ease,
> The wounded spirit heal.
>
> May we in faith receive thy word,
> In faith present our prayers,
> And in the presence of our Lord
> Unbosom all our cares.
>
> (J. Newton, 1769.)

10. THE GOSPEL VERSUS LEGALISM

Acts, Chapter 26, vv. 9-15

I verily thought with myself, that I ought to do many things contrary to the name of Jesus of Nazareth. And this I also did in Jerusalem: and I both shut up many of the saints in prisons, having received authority from the chief priests, and when they were put to death, I gave my vote against them. And punishing them oftentimes in all the synagogues, I strove to make them blaspheme; and being exceedingly mad against them, I persecuted them even unto foreign cities. Whereupon as I journeyed to Damascus with the authority and commission of the chief priests, at midday, O king, I saw on the way a light from heaven, above the brightness of the sun, shining round about me and them that journeyed with me. And when we were all fallen to the earth, I heard a voice saying unto me in the Hebrew language, Saul, Saul, why persecutest thou me? It is hard for thee to kick against the goad. And I said, Who art thou, Lord? And the Lord said, I am Jesus whom thou persecutest.

ACTS 26, v. 14: Saul, Saul, why persecutest thou me? It is hard for thee to kick against the goad.

YOU won't misunderstand me if I say I have wanted to ask that question myself. I have wanted to ask of some person or persons (not acquainted with the Church)—why do you seize upon every opportunity to try and expose my religious faith? Why do you wish to engage me in open debate before other people? Why do you not leave me alone? Can it be that you are afraid of my religion? Can it be that you fear it may

198

be alive after all, and true after all, and right and proper for all men after all? The fact is no one kicks a dead dog! Does not your very hostility show that you sense there is life in my faith?

Forgive me for speaking personally. Believe me, I only do so for clarity's sake in lighting up my subject this morning—"Saul, Saul, why persecutest thou me?" But what are you afraid of? Why are you so mad against the Christians? Why do you torture them, making them blaspheme and so incriminate them in the courts? Why do you imprison them? Why don't you leave them alone? What are you afraid of? Why this mad rush to Damascus to root them out like vermin? What can a few harmless men and a handful of women do to you? Look in your own soul, Saul! Where is the bogy? Is he really outside in Damascus, or is he perchance inside you peering at you through the eyes of your own soul?

When people get mad against religion, they are strong witnesses to the truth of religion—which is why St. Paul has become one of the most powerful witnesses Christianity ever had. And now people are mad against him! They try to explain him away! Listen to them—Saul suffered sunstroke on the Damascus Road! Saul underwent an hallucination on the Damascus Road! And his theology is out of alignment with the teaching of Jesus. And his outlook on life? It is jaundiced; sour-mouthed; and utterly repressed! He was a dry intellectual; he was a time-server! He was a busybody in other men's matters! Any stick men pick up now with which to beat the Apostle Paul. And you ask why? And I ask why? Can it be his enemies sense the truth of all that came to him on the Damascus Road? After all, you do not kick a dead dog!

* * *

Let us look for a moment at Saul on the Damascus Road. He is a goaded man. Something is getting at him. Memories are getting at him. They won't leave him alone. And the more he kicks the more they hurt. First, I shouldn't wonder —the failure of Judaism to give him peace of mind. James

Stewart in his book *A Man in Christ* sets this out so very clearly. You see, the essence of Judaism is Pelagian. You work out your own salvation; you tot up an account with God of all your prayers, of all your almsgivings, and all your kindly thoughts and ways. More than that, if God has set us laws of life you set your hope on all the times that you have kept his laws. . . . There have been lapses, of course. There have been sins, of course. There has been the adulterous look. There has been the cruel act. But you hope that in the end, when the great book-keeping God (up there) makes up the final score, your good deeds will out-balance all that might be set against you, and so God will take you to your final home—that is legalism in religion. And legalism is the heart of Judaism. And it's hard work. And uncertain work, because, of course, you never know till the books are opened whether you have "passed" or not.

All this goaded Saul on the Damascus Road. It had been goading him for months. Can legalism be right? Can God be a book-keeper? Is there no peace of mind *now*? And hope now? And eternal life now? . . . And because he feared he might be wrong, Saul kicked his way against the goad— "Saul, Saul, why persecutest thou me?"

* * *

A second goad, I shouldn't wonder, was the fact of Christ. Christ is still an uncommonly sharp goad in life. He takes an extraordinary amount of explaining away. And Saul never did explain him away. In spite of II Corinthians 5, v. 16, I often wonder if he ever met him. Was Saul there, as a student perhaps, in the last week of shattering debate in the Temple courts between Jesus and his foes? Shattering because Jesus slipped them in the pincer-movement questions, and then attacked them with all the whip an argument can unleash. Was Saul at the back of the court when Caiaphas held him there on trial? Did Saul attend by the Cross himself, wagging his head and crying: "Ha! thou that destroyed the Temple, save thyself and us." If so, did Saul of Tarsus see him die? Did he perchance hear, or overhear, those words of Jesus:

"Father, forgive them for they know not what they do"?
Did he ever forget what he saw? Did he ever forget what he
overheard? After all, it pierced the callousness of the Roman
centurion on guard—"Truly this was a righteous man." I
do not know the answer to these questions. But the Sanhedrin
had spies on Jesus. And they had files on Jesus. And they
had memories of Jesus, vivid memories; and Saul would
know its members well. He would know of those reports.
And then on the Damascus Road, with every clip-clop,
clip-clop, clip-clop of the horse's hoofs, the fact of Christ,
the fact of Christ, the fact of Christ dinned itself into his
soul—"Saul, Saul, why persecutest thou me? It is hard for
thee to kick against the goad."

*　　*　　*

And then the Christians. You don't push innocent men
and women into filthy oriental dungeons without them doing
something to your soul. The first victim of hate is not him
who is hated, but he who hates. And when your victims turn
and bless you and pray for you who despitefully use them,
asking God to open your eyes to see the folly of your ways—
how do you sleep after that? How do you think after that?
How do you go your way as if the world were any kind of
lovely place? And so with every clip-clop, clip-clop, clip-clop
of the horse's hoofs upon the Damascus road some man's
face, some woman's face, some Christian face with a cry on
the lips breaking into a prayer bit deeper into his soul.
Could these Christians be wrong? Could their Christ be
false? Could their faith be one huge damnable lie? Saul was
all but at breaking point. . . .

*　　*　　*

And still another goad. A man with the face of an angel.
A man with a prayer on his lips, "Lord, lay not this sin to
their charge." And Saul stood there on the hillside as his
fellow-members of the Jewish court hurled down stones till
he was dead—a crumpled mass without his clothes, his
clothes deposited in a pile by Saul's own feet. Stephanos was

his name, which means "a crown". Could Saul doubt that he had won his crown of life?

*   *   *

"Saul, Saul, why persecutest thou me? It is hard for thee to kick against the goad." Oh, you haven't explained an experience when you have analysed its component parts. The onus still remains to show why Saul of Tarsus was converted. Were the roots of the experience subjective or were they objective? Did it happen because of something in his inner consciousness, or did something happen in his inner consciousness because of a Power completely other than himself? St. Paul took the latter view. He said *Christ* appeared to him on the Damascus Road. "Appeared" to him—a word in Greek used of the resurrection appearance of Jesus. So Christ is alive. Christ is real. Christ is God. Such was Paul's abiding conviction—"Saul, Saul, why persecutest thou me? It is hard for thee to kick against the goads. And I said, Who art thou Lord? And the Lord said, I am Jesus whom thou persecutest."

*   *   *

And someone says—we do not have these experiences these days. Most Church-people could not point to such a climax in their faith. I know that, my friend. And if there are theologians present I too know what Johannes Weiss wrote in *Das Urchristentum*. It *is* true Peter is the rock foundation of the Church, not Paul. It *is* true most of us came to the Cross by way of Galilee like all the Apostles, not by way of the Damascus Road—I did myself. We asked—what shall we do with our lives? And nurtured in the Christian traditions we went on to follow Christ—and so he led us to Calvary. It was a gradual illumination. But look! this is the universal element in St. Paul's experience which is the bed rock of all Christian experience—we cannot save ourselves.

> Could my zeal no respite know,
> Could my tears for ever flow,
> All for sin could not atone:
> Thou must save, and thou alone.

That is the gospel over against legalism. That is the faith which lifts a man up, turns him round and sets his feet on the right road. Let us understand the truth. Let us commit ourselves to this Lord. Then indeed we have a faith to sing about. "Praise the Lord, O my soul, and all that is within me praise his holy name."

11. THE MORE EXCELLENT WAY

I Corinthians, Chapter 12, v. 31; Chapter 13, vv. 1-13

But desire earnestly the greater gifts. And a still more excellent way show I unto you.

If I speak with the tongues of men and of angels, but have not love, I am become sounding brass, or a clanging cymbal. And if I have the gift of prophecy, and know all mysteries and all knowledge; and if I have all faith, so as to remove mountains, but have not love, I am nothing. And if I bestow all my goods to feed the poor, and if I give my body to be burned, but have not love, it profiteth me nothing. Love suffereth long, and is kind; love envieth not; love vaunteth not itself, is not puffed up, doth not behave itself unseemly, seeketh not its own, is not provoked, taketh not account of evil; rejoiceth not in unrighteousness, but rejoiceth with the truth; beareth all things, believeth all things, hopeth all things, endureth all things. Love never faileth: but whether there be prophecies, they shall be done away; whether there be tongues, they shall cease; whether there be knowledge, it shall be done away. For we know in part, and we prophesy in part: but when that which is perfect is come, that which is in part shall be done away. When I was a child, I spake as a child, I felt as a child, I thought as a child: now that I am become a man, I have put away childish things. For now we see in a mirror, darkly; but then face to face: now I know in part; but then shall I know even as also I have been known. But now abideth faith, hope, love, these three; and the greatest of these is love.

I CORINTHIANS 12, v. 31: But desire earnestly the greater gifts. And a still more excellent way show I unto you.

I WONDER what you would do if you were a Bishop? Perhaps you think that is a stupid question. . . . But I wonder what you would do if you were faced with the fact that the Church of England is losing six hundred clergy every year through death and retirement, and only about four hundred new men are coming in? What would you do? You see, more than the number required do actually apply for acceptance; that is to say, there could be enough men to fill all the posts. There *could* be; that is to say, if the present standards were lowered and little attention were paid to the passing of examinations. What would *you* do? Would you count it a matter of importance that the clergy should possess some gifts? Or would you be satisfied that the candidates were kindly men?

I would hazard a guess that you would hesitate before you gave your answer. In all probability, I think you would suggest that a potential clergyman ought perhaps to possess something of a gift for public speaking. I would have thought so myself. Preaching has been treated in a very casual fashion by the clergy in modern times, typified perhaps by the curate who asked his Vicar what he should preach about, and the reply was, "Preach about God, and preach about ten minutes."

Then I would have thought a clergyman ought to be something of a scholar. I hesitate to say that the standard of education has advanced in the country as a whole to any very great extent, but there will certainly be no Christian influence brought to bear upon the leaders of the community unless the clergy are to some degree learned men. . . .

Furthermore, I would have thought the clergy ought to be men who can get things done. After all, unless the leader in a church has vision, faith, enterprise, and energy, the place will never boast more than a mere handful of worshippers, an unbalanced budget, and a dilapidated set of buildings. There are mountains to be removed these days in all Church work, and vigour is required to tackle them.

But then I take up St. Paul's letter: "If I speak with the tongues of men and of angels, but have not love, I am become sounding brass or a clanging cymbal." How depressing! All these years to master the art of preaching and

Paul dubs it "emission of noise". And what is his comment on scholarship? . . . and no man is a scholar without blood, sweat, toil, and tears. "And if I have the gift of prophesy and know all mysteries and all knowledge . . . I am nothing." How discouraging!

And what of the third gift I would have counted necessary —energy to get things done? "And if I have all faith so as to remove mountains, but have not love, I am nothing. . . ."

As it happens, St. Paul throws in two other gifts which I omitted, but he marks them down with the same definiteness: "And though I bestow all my goods to feed the poor," in other words, almsgiving to the uttermost; furthermore, even if I become a martyr to the Christian cause: "and though I give my body to be burned"; some Christians in the Emperor Nero's reign had to do this, they had their bodies tarred, were slung up on poles, and set alight for the purpose of illuminating the Imperial gardens at night—"and though I give my body to be burned, but have not love, it profiteth me nothing."

O Paul, what do you mean? What *can* you mean? Do you want a Church led by nincompoops? And filled with nincompoops? Is this guidance the bishops must follow—to pay no attention to examinations whatsoever? No attention to standards? No attention to gifts? O Paul, can't we have gifted men in the pulpit, and gifted hearers in the pew?

But look a little closer. It isn't true that St. Paul discourages gifts. He writes in fact: "Desire earnestly the greater gifts." Nor does he allege that gifts are ineffective, he asserts that their possessors may *be* nothing. Nor does he suggest that almsgiving and life-giving do not profit someone, but they do not profit the donor. All gifts are valueless in the absence of love. It is love that makes the gifts worth while, Christian love.

And haven't you tested this for yourself? Have you never heard a speaker whose words flow from his lips like water from a tap, but he is not moved, and you are not moved? And have you no experience of scholars, Christian scholars, scholars in the Christian ministry, dry and dull to a deadly

206

degree? And who hasn't met administrators, administrators in the Church, organisers, men who get things done; but when your heart is breaking and the light of your life has gone out—and sooner or later these things come to us all—you turn down a side street, mount a bus, plunge into a shop, you do anything to avoid the competent administrator when you see him approaching . . . But the effective preacher who has love, the scholar who has love, the administrator who has love, ah, that is different, *he* is different, you do not avoid meeting him!

I remember years ago now, when I was given my first church, writing to one of the most able men in the Church of England, inviting him to come and preach in my pulpit. It was a daring thing to do. In those early days, my church was a struggling one, and I was not in the least surprised that he did not come. But he wrote such a kindly refusal, conveying such a spirit of humility and graciousness (he even thanked me for asking him, I have never forgotten that!), with the result that I am sure his postcard has had more lasting influence on me than any sermon. I have paid attention to him ever since.

It is love which makes the other gifts effective. We need the gifts. We need the preachers. We need the scholars. We need the administrators. We need them all very badly in the Church of England just now. "Desire earnestly the greater gifts," wrote St. Paul. Yet this is what he went on to say, "And a still more excellent way show I unto you—If I speak with the tongues of men and of angels but have not love, I am become sounding brass or a clanging cymbal." It is love which makes the other gifts effective.

* * *

But what is this love? Strange to say, we do not possess a word for it in English. "Love" will not really do, it is too broad. Neither will "charity" (as in the Authorised Version), it is too narrow. That subtle tongue, Greek, possessed a number of words for "love". The first was EROS, represented by that statue in Piccadilly Circus which has such a strange attraction for drunks on New Year's Eve. EROS is sexual love. It is desire. It is the passion which must possess. I *must* have, that is EROS. It seeks self-satisfaction. Obviously this is not Paul's more excellent way.

Then there was PHILIA. We have it in words like Philadelphia, Philanthropy, Anglophile. It means "friendship" or "sociability". It means loving in the sense of "liking"—I like human beings, I like Englishmen.

Then there was a forgotten word. Scarcely anybody used it. But the Christians used it. They brought it up out of the lumber room and wrote it across the pages of their writings. It was the word AGAPE. It is not "I want, I must have, I must get satisfaction from" (which is EROS), it is "I must give, I must help, I must make the other person happy"— AGAPE, or, in the matchless words of St. Paul: "It suffereth long, and is kind; love envieth not; love vaunteth not itself, is not puffed up, doth not behave itself unseemly, seeketh not its own, is not provoked, taketh not account of evil; rejoiceth not in unrighteousness, but rejoiceth with the truth; beareth all things, believeth all things, hopeth all things, endureth all things. AGAPE never faileth. . . ."

And someone says, "Oh, if only there were more people in the world like that!" But *God* is like that. This is what the New Testament teaches. Not of course if you accept a Unitarian view of God. Not if you accept no Incarnation, no coming of God in the flesh "for us men and for our salvation". Then Jesus was merely a good man; albeit, a *very* good man, but still in no essential way different from us. Oh, no, God cannot be accepted as a God of Love in face of all the heartbreaks there are in life if he never has done anything about it but stay in heaven. But the Christian's view is that God has come, and Christ is God. So that God *is* Love.

And don't you see that what really makes God God is not all his other attributes—his almightiness, his holiness, his eternity, his omnipresence. It is love. If in the case of preachers, scholars, and administrators it is love which makes their gifts effective, of course it is the same with God. God cannot be less than man. God must therefore be Love.

And this is what sustains a man whose way is hard. This is what enables a woman to continue even if her life is empty of the experiences she would long to have. In face of tragedy, brokenness, and frailty, the conviction that somehow God is Love has enabled countless thousands to face their lot. And not merely with dumb resignation, but with willing co-operation.

This is the heart of the matter. God is Love—AGAPE. And if, too, you have a human friend, some man, some woman, in whom is reflected the love of God, what a source of strength you possess! Do not lose him, do not lose her. It is those in whom AGAPE dwells who sustain life. And if you ask me why, I could only reply in the words of St. Paul which would be most appropriate on Quinquagesima Sunday —Love never faileth; but whether there be prophecies, they shall be done away; whether there be tongues, they shall cease; whether there be knowledge, it shall vanish away. For we know in part and we prophesy in part: but when that which is perfect is come, then that which is in part shall be done away.... And now abideth faith, hope, AGAPE, these three; and the greatest of these is AGAPE.

12. THE HUMAN IN THE DIVINE

PHILIPPIANS, CHAPTER 2, VV. 5-11

Have this mind in you, which was also in Christ Jesus: who being in the form of God, counted it not a prize to be on an equality with God, but emptied himself, taking the form of a servant, being made in the likeness of men; and being found in fashion as a man, he humbled himself, becoming obedient even unto death, yea, the death of the cross.

Wherefore also God highly exalted him, and gave unto him the name which is above every name; that in the name of Jesus every knee should bow, of things in heaven and things on earth and things under the earth. And that every tongue should confess that Jesus Christ is Lord, to the glory of God the Father.

∞∞∞∞∞∞∞∞∞∞∞∞∞∞∞∞∞∞∞∞∞∞∞

PHILIPPIANS 2, v. 9: Wherefore also God highly exalted him.

∞∞∞∞∞∞∞∞∞∞∞∞∞∞∞∞∞∞∞∞∞∞∞

I WONDER if you've ever had a friend, perhaps someone with whom you've worked and talked and laughed, and then suddenly he was elevated to some exalted position? I've had that happen to me more than once. How did you feel about it? Did you resent the elevation? Were you *opposed* to the elevation? I don't think you were, were you? If you thought your friend was worthy of it, if he had spent himself in sacrificial labour without one thought of the rewards that might come his way, but only of what he was doing for other people. You even rejoiced in his elevation. You thought he deserved it.

Now this morning, at this Ascension-tide, it is my duty,

and my privilege, to turn your thoughts to our Lord's elevation. Did it ever occur to you, I wonder, that he deserved it? And you think that is an odd way to put it. But that is how St. Paul put it. Listen! "And being found in fashion as a man, he humbled himself, becoming obedient unto death, yea, the death of the cross. Wherefore also God highly exalted him . . ."—he deserved it—". . . and gave him the name which is above every name."

Oh, I know that Calvin found this idea quite unacceptable; but then Calvin found quite a number of truths which have nourished other people unacceptable! He positively wriggled to avoid this one. He affirmed that the Greek word διὸ means "quo facto", which is nonsense. The Greek can fairly be translated as Phillips translates it—"(Christ) humbled himself by living a life of utter obedience, even to the extent of dying and the death he died was that of a common criminal. That is why God has now lifted him so high. . . ."

And then some scholars have quarrelled over this word "exalted". It is ὑπερύψωσε. They've said it doesn't refer to the Ascension at all, but to the Resurrection. In fact some have bent over backwards to affirm that there is no firm testimony to Our Lord's Ascension anywhere in the scriptures. The Resurrection is the Ascension!

I don't want you to think all this tradition of Our Lord's Ascension is plain sailing to me. Far from it. I'm a twentieth-century man as much as you, perhaps more when it comes to theology! I've had to come to terms with what we recite every Sunday in the Creed—"He descended into hell, He ascended into heaven." You see, I can't believe in a 3-decker universe—Hell in the basement, Earth on the ground floor, and Heaven in the attic, any more than you can. And I have a strong suspicion that that is precisely what our New Testament writers believed, *and* the authors of our Christian Creeds.

But I'm not going to explain the Ascension by explaining it away! I'm not going to say the Ascension is really the Resurrection. I'm going to say straight out that I believe we should accept the Ascension as a symbol. It means that after his resurrection Jesus was exalted to a new level of being. He returned to the divine mode of existence.

So you can abandon if you like those antiquated representations of the Ascension sometimes seen in stained-glass windows, which make you laugh as much as they make me laugh, especially that one of a pair of feet dangling from a cloud and two solid footprints in the sand beneath—and that is the Ascension!

Let such pictures go. De-mythologise the whole episode if you like, and if you like that word "de-mythologise". But don't say there was no such event as the Ascension, and don't say it stands for no great spiritual truth. It does. Because Christ humbled himself, he was exalted. This is what Jesus himself taught: "He that humbleth himself shall be exalted." And St. Paul said (pace Calvin) he deserved that elevation. "And being found in fashion as a man, he humbled himself, wherefore also God highly exalted him." In other words—oh, I know they are strong, but the Ascension is the reward of the Incarnation—

> The highest place that heav'n affords
> Is His, is His by right,
> The King of Kings and Lord of Lords,
> And heav'n's eternal Light.
>
> (T. Kelly, 1820.)

But what can the Ascension mean for people living in London to-day?

A short time ago there was consecrated in Southwark Cathedral a new bishop. I haven't met him, but I know there has been a good deal of discussion about his clothes and his political affiliations. But I prayed for him. All Church people ought to pray for any elevated to episcopal rank. And of this I am certain, that in Southwark there will be a large number of hard-pressed clergy labouring in desperately difficult dock-side parishes who will be grateful that one occupies the episcopal throne there who has himself laboured for years in dockland and understands their problems.

And that is what Our Lord's Ascension means to

Londoners now, and to people everywhere else. That the occupant of the Eternal Throne of Heaven understands our human problems.

One of our problems is that we do not know what is coming to us, whether good, bad, or (what is perhaps worse) plain mediocrity. And so we don't know what plans to make, what adjustments; all we can do is go on day after day, sometimes in the darkness, doing what comes to hand. And all this makes God seem very remote till we remember that Our Lord lived like this. He did not know what lay in store for him when he closed the carpenter's shop door for the last time and set forth as an itinerant preacher. He did not know what plots the scribes were hatching when they hearkened to his preaching. He did not know when the trap would close and he find himself on a public gallows. Instead, he had what we all have—forebodings and presentiments. And now he occupies the Eternal Throne, and I am glad there is One there who knows how I feel, who knows my problems. I rejoice, therefore, in the Ascension. It gives me confidence in the humanity of God.

And someone is startled. The humanity of God! Yes, that *is* what I said. And you thought, didn't you, that divinity and humanity were opposites, poles apart like positive and negative in electricity. And it isn't true. The Ascension cries from the housetops that it isn't true. The human Jesus ascended to the divine throne.

Oh, how I laughed inside myself the other day when I was calling on an elderly lady and she said, "You know, sometimes I think God must be very human." I laughed because she would have been the last person to admit to theological thinking. But it was theological thinking, profound theological thinking. You can find it set out in a book called *The Divine and the Human* by Nicolas Berdyaev, a very profound Russian theologian.

You see, if it is true that men are divine, it is also true that God is human. And because there is divinity in manhood, and humanity in divinity, there is a bond between them both. And to set this out in black and white God became a man—

213

that is the Incarnation. And to set it out in black and white a second time, man re-occupied the Divine Throne, that is the Ascension . . . since when you won't be able to say any more, and I won't be able to say any more, that God doesn't understand me, and I cannot know God.

Understanding! What a wonderful gift that is. I remember years ago meeting the late Bishop Duppuy of Hong Kong. He was no theologian, neither (I'm afraid) was he much of a preacher. I can see him now struggling with the preparation of a sermon, and I shouldn't wonder if the congregation didn't have to struggle when they listened. Butsee him with people! I saw him in a guest house with about fifty total strangers. But they weren't strangers for long. It was only a matter of days before he had talked to everyone, and only a few days more before they were telling him their troubles. The fact was, he never made you feel of no consequence, or stupid, or completely outside the pale. He seemed to know by instinct just what you felt and just what you needed. And you wondered how, and where, he had gained this remarkable human understanding, till you learned how hard life had been for him. . . .

And this is the message of the Ascension. Not some strange and difficult theological speculation (though sometimes we have to engage in this), but that the God who reigns on high is full of human understanding. Why? Because he himself knew tiredness, he himself was tempted, he himself once trod the daily round we all are forced to tread. In fact, "He emptied himself, taking the form of a servant, being made in the likeness of men; and being found in fashion as a man he humbled himself, becoming obedient even unto death, yea, the death of the Cross. Wherefore also God highly exalted him. . . ."

Am I addressing myself to someone who is finding the Christian faith difficult of acceptance? Perhaps you have a science training and find our lack of proofs a major stumbling block. Perhaps your marriage has broken, and you are "put off" by the Church's attitude to divorce. Maybe you have even grown out of touch with most aspects of religion, and, if the truth were told, you find it all a little dull. My friend, this is what I'd like to say to you—it is the message of the Ascension: God knows how you feel. Don't be put off, our God is a God of perfect human understanding. There is a place for you, there is a faith for you. No one need imagine that he is left outside and will not be acceptable. This is the Ascension message—our God is very, very human. . . .

13. A DOOR IN HEAVEN

REVELATION, CHAPTER 4, VV. 1-6; CHAPTER 5, VV. 1-11

After these things I saw, and behold, a door opened in heaven, and the first voice which I heard, a voice as of a trumpet speaking with me, one saying, come up hither, and I will shew thee the things which must come to pass hereafter. Straightway I was in the Spirit: and behold, there was a throne set in heaven, and one sitting upon the throne; and he that sat was to look upon like a jasper stone and a sardius: and there was a rainbow round about the throne, like an emerald to look upon. And round about the throne were four and twenty thrones: and upon the thrones I saw four and twenty elders sitting, arrayed in white garments; and on their heads crowns of gold. And out of the throne proceed lightnings and voices and thunders. And there were seven lamps of fire burning before the throne, which are the seven Spirits of God; and before the throne, as it were a glassy sea like unto crystal; and in the midst of the throne, and round about the throne, four living creatures full of eyes before and behind.

And I saw in the right hand of him that sat on the throne a book written within and on the back, close sealed with seven seals. And I saw a strong angel proclaiming with a great voice, Who is worthy to open the book, and to loose the seals thereof? And no one in the heaven, or on the earth, or under the earth, was able to open the book, or to look thereon. And I wept much, because no one was found worthy to open the book, or to look thereon: and one of the elders saith unto me, Weep not: behold, the Lion that is of the tribe of Judah, the Root of David, hath overcome, to open the book and the seven seals thereof. And I saw in the midst of the throne and of the four living creatures, and in the midst of the elders, a Lamb standing, as though it had been slain, having seven horns, and seven eyes, which are the seven Spirits of God, sent forth into all the earth. And he came,

216

and he taketh it out of the right hand of him that sat on the throne. And when he had taken the book, the four living creatures and the four and twenty elders fell down before the Lamb, having each one a harp, and golden bowls full of incense, which are the prayers of the saints. And they sing a new song, saying, Worthy art thou to take the book, and to open the seals thereof: for thou wast slain, and didst purchase unto God with thy blood men of every tribe, and tongue, and people, and nation, and madest them to be unto our God a kingdom and priests; and they reign upon the earth.

And I saw, and I heard a voice of many angels round about the throne and the living creatures and the elders; and the number of them was ten thousand times ten thousand, and thousands of thousands.

REVELATION 4, v. 1: After this I looked, and, behold, a door was opened in heaven.

WHEN you enter the baroque churches in Bavaria, you gasp as you are meant to gasp. You see in the architecture a picture overspilling the frame, you see the exception leaping up to be the rule. You see the utter and complete, yes, almost fantastic, counterpart of the classical which is conformity to law and order. Here is the counter-reformation. Here is the last bid for the capture of the human spirit through the senses instead of through the reason, as in the Aufklärung. Baroque is spectacular, theatrical, even a show, because it tries to tell us that all this world is all a passing show. It strains after *un*realism in a world of realism. And if you look at every baroque ceiling you will see a door supposed to open into heaven—it is our final destiny from out this passing show.

"After this I looked, and, behold, a door was opened in heaven." Last Monday morning before breakfast, I walked by "the round pond". I scarcely saw another person, the park was quite deserted. And as a flight of wild duck skimmed the water making for the Serpentine, and the sun broke through a

217

bank of clouds colouring the trees, the stillness, the scenery, and the sounding of a distant bell became a door for me opening into heaven, more than the Latin prayer-book left upon my desk which I so often use. Then it was this text came to my mind: "After this I looked, and, behold, a door was opened in heaven." And it struck me—not for John the writer of the Revelation was some peaceful scene his door opening into heaven, but a concentration camp upon the isle of Patmos and forced labour, cruel labour, labour in the quarries, labour till you died.

And there he stood that sabbath morning looking to the mainland. That mainland where that very morning men would gather in their churches—Ephesus, Smyrna, Pergamum, Thyatira, Sardia, Philadelphia, Laodicea. And Domitian might wreck them, Domitian issuing edicts from his throne in Rome, edicts formed to crush the little Church, the only body in the Empire that dared withstand the worship of the Caesar. What would be the outcome? . . . the outcome in a thousand years? . . . the outcome in the final reckoning? And as John thought about those Churches and the Caesar on his throne, he said "After this I looked, and, behold, a door was opened in heaven." Or if you want this all in black and white, chapters 1 to 3 of the Revelation deal with the things that are upon this earth, chapters 5 and 6 take us to the scenes behind the door of heaven; and, after that, from chapter 6, the things which shall be in the future.

* * *

"After this I looked, and, behold, a door was opened in heaven." What did John see? First, a throne. Not the Imperial throne, but God's throne, the throne which Isaiah saw and Daniel saw, coloured perhaps with Babylonian astrology. But in seeing this through the door in heaven, the seer knew no earthly potentate would have the final word. There is a King of Kings and Lord of Lords, and no Domitian, Ivan the Terrible, Bonaparte, or Hitler is the master of our destinies.

I did not think of all this in the park last Monday morning, but I thought of it when I came back home and read this book, the Revelation, the last book in the Bible. And I thought how God is King of my time and your time, of my life and your life. And how I ought not to fear and you ought not to fear. And how I ought not to be disobedient and you ought not to be disobedient. Whatever kings may seem to dominate —financial kings, big business kings, fashion kings and political kings—the real King is the King of kings, and he cares for human beings.

* * *

"After this I looked, and, behold, a door was opened in heaven." What did John see? Living creatures full of eyes before and behind. Eyes, mark you! Eyes which saw the churches on the mainland. Eyes which saw the Emperor strutting in his palace. Eyes which saw his prisoner bent in Patmos, bent in cruel chains, bent beneath the blows of warders' batons beating to the quarries.

Oh, you've never lived if you don't know what it means to be thankful for the eyes of God. Does no one know? Does no one see? Does no one care about this plight of mine? "After this I looked, and, behold, a door was opened in heaven," and then I saw the living creatures full of eyes at back and front. "Omniscience" is the Latin way we turn this Hebrew thought. But what an uplift! What an infinite consolation! Though no one seems to see the injustices I face, I am alone and no one seems to care. But God sees and God cares, and he is final King. One day you will be justified.

* * *

"After this I looked, and, behold, a door was opened in heaven." It was an Old Testament scene up there, an Old Testament divine court, and Old Testament symbolism and imagery. Not that this makes it any less the truth. In all the world before Messiah came, there was no truth so clearly seen as in the Jewish Testament. But it wasn't the whole truth, it wasn't the complete truth about our human situation. John knew it looking through the door that opened in heaven.

And so he wept, wept when he saw no man worthy to open the book, the book of human destiny (chapter 5, v. 4). And then he saw again one standing in the midst of living creatures, a Lamb slain to whom the book was given. After which the chorus rose on high: "Worthy art thou to take the book, and to open and read thereof, for thou wast slain and didst purchase for God with thy blood men of every tribe and tongue and people and nation, and madest them to be unto our God a kingdom of priests: and they reign upon the earth."

So John saw the Christian interpretation of history. It is Christ who carries out the purposes of God. It is Christ in whom the purposes of God for man are finally understandable. Christ the lion of Judah, but Christ a sacrificial lamb. God reigns, but he reigns through the sacrifice of love, the outcropping of which eternal fact is seen in history at the place called Calvary. And so the Christ is elevated to the throne—"Worthy is the Lamb that was slain to receive power and riches and wisdom and might and honour and glory and blessing." So that if you ever wish to know the revolution necessary in a Jewish mind, like John's, for it to be fully Christian, you ought to read this book. "A door was opened in heaven" and he saw *Jesus* on the throne, Jesus co-equal with God. So says the Revelation.

* * *

"A door was opened in heaven." We never know when that will happen. It may be in the park when walking by the "round pond". It may be as you sit alone thinking of your circumstances. It may be—how I wish it could be—here in Church, for this would justify my ministry.

"After this I looked, and, behold, a door was opened in heaven." When this happens, we shall always see God in control of all that is, God with eyes, who knows us through and through, and Christ the one through whom God reaches us. This is Christian revelation, and the result is always Christian poise.